THE
GRATEFUL DEAD

TRIVIA QUIZ

THE
GRATEFUL DEAD

TRIVIA QUIZ

by
MARK KNICKELBINE

BowerHouseBooks.com

Cover Design by Margaret McCullough
Text Design by Rebecca Finkel
Printed in Canada

Library of Congress Control Number: 2008925363

Paperback ISBN: 978-1-934553-06-0

10 9 8 7 6 5 4 3 2

TABLE OF
CONTENTS

CHAPTER ONE

"On the day that I was born ..." 1

CHAPTER TWO

Mother McCree's Uptown Jug Champions 25

CHAPTER THREE

The Rainbow Explodes 49

CHAPTER FOUR

Doin' the New Speedway Boogie 81

CHAPTER FIVE

Uncle John's Band 109

CHAPTER SIX

So Many Roads 143

After years of playing the folk music circuit in the Bay Area, Bill Kreutzman, Jerry Garcia, Phil Lesh, Bob Weir, and Ron McKernan grew their hair, picked up electric guitars and became a rock band.

CHAPTER ONE

"On the day that I was born . . ."

The Depression was over, the War was over, and Americans had never had it so good. The generation that had seen such hard times in the '30s and '40s were now ready to pursue their dream: prosperity and leisure in a little home of their own. And in the 1950s, California was the epicenter of the American Dream, the golden shore where you could go to find the good life and reinvent yourself in any style you liked. And even if the leisure was a little silly, the music a little slick, the suburban lifestyle a little regimented—hey, it was still the greatest life anybody had ever had.

The kids who grew up in those pastel suburban bungalows were the first to believe that the sky was the limit, that in America you could go anywhere your imagination could take you. And there were endless things to feed your imagination, especially in a place like San Francisco, where the avant garde of art, music, and the bohemian lifestyle was close at hand. It was a time and place where a kid could dream of escaping the dreary world of nine-to-five careers, Red Scare politics, and atom bombs and go to the land of comic books and rock 'n' roll. Into this world were born a handful of boys to dream the dreams, boys who would grow up to lead their generation to places their parents could never have imagined.

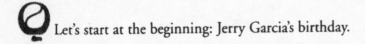
Q Let's start at the beginning: Jerry Garcia's birthday.

A Jerome John Garcia was born on August 1, 1942, at Children's Hospital in San Francisco. It was five days before the United States dropped the first nuclear bomb on Japan.

Q So what would that make his astrological sign?

A Leo, with Libra rising. Leos are known for their creativity and natural talent for organization. Pluto was in the Tenth House when Jerry was born, auspicious for a forceful personality; Jupiter was in the Ninth House, associated with outgoing and optimistic people; and the moon in the Sixth House raises concerns about sickness and health. Freaky, huh?

Q Who were Jerry's parents?

A Jose "Joe" Garcia, the son of Spanish immigrants, who spent most of his adult life tending bar, and Ruth Marie "Bobbie" Clifford, a nurse of Swedish and Irish extraction.

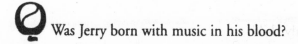

Q Was Jerry born with music in his blood?

A Certainly. His father was a clarinetist who fronted his own jazz bands before a dispute with the musician's union ended his musical career. Jerry would remember his dad playing his clarinet to lull him to sleep. Bobbie, along with being a devotee of astrology and spiritualism, was a student of opera and played the piano.

Q Who was little Jerry named after?

A Jerome Kern, his mother's favorite composer.

Q What was young Jerry's first musical obsession?

A At about four years old, he discovered an old wind-up Victrola in his grandmother's attic, along with a box of dusty old records of traditional songs (the term "folk song" had yet to enter the popular lexicon). The boy figured out how to make the machine work, and proceeded to play the records over and over again, testing the sanity of his family.

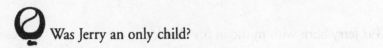

Q Was Jerry an only child?

A No. His brother Clifford, nicknamed "Tiff," was five years his senior.

Q Everyone knows Jerry was missing most of the middle finger on his right hand. How did it happen?

A In the spring of 1947, Tiff was chopping wood at their grandparents' house; his little brother was trying to help. The axe removed Jerry's finger below the second joint. Characteristically, his most powerful memory of the event was a sound: the buzzing in his ears as he went into shock.

Q Jerry was to suffer an even greater loss later that same year. What happened?

A While on a family vacation in northern California, Joe Garcia drowned in a fishing accident. Jerry later claimed to have witnessed his father's death from the shore.

Q Jerry Garcia's posthumously-published visual autobiography is entitled *Harrington Street*. To what does the title refer?

A The tavern and rooming house his father established, called Joe Garcia's, was located at the corner of 1st and Harrington streets, near the San Francisco waterfront. After his father's death, his mother ran the place, and young Jerry spent a good deal of his childhood in the neighborhood.

Q Was Jerry good in school?

A Alas, no. His teachers and friends recognized that he was one of the brightest kids in his class; but despite his occasional success at subjects that interested him, and his brief stint in a fast-learner program, he was generally an indifferent student and had to repeat the eighth grade. He ran with the tough crowd on Harrington Street, kids who introduced him to two lifelong interests: marijuana and rock 'n' roll.

Q What was Jerry's first musical instrument?

A He had the usual abortive piano lessons as a child. As he approached his fifteenth birthday, he pestered his mother to buy him a guitar. Bobbie gave him an accordion instead.

Q So did Jerry become a polka king?

A No; the boy demanded that they take the accordion to a local pawn shop to swap it for a Danelectro guitar he had his eye on. He got his wish.

Q Who taught Jerry Garcia to play the guitar?

A Chuck Berry, sort of. Actually, Jerry taught himself to play the guitar by listening to Chuck Berry records on the bar juke box and trying to imitate what he heard.

Q Avant garde artist Wally Hedrick was well known in the Bay Area in the mid-'50s. What was his greatest contribution to San Francisco culture?

A Even though he was a driving force behind the famous Six Gallery poetry reading in 1955 at which Allan Ginsberg introduced his magnum opus, *Howl,* Hedrick's greatest act arguably was introducing Jerry Garcia to the bohemian scene in San Francisco. Hedrick was on the faculty of the California School of Fine Arts, which had a Saturday outreach program for high school students; Jerry attended it to nurture his skills as a painter. The two connected and Hedrick hipped Garcia to the North Beach coffeehouse scene, Lawrence Ferlinghetti's City Lights Bookstore, and Jack Kerouac's *On the Road.* It was an environment that would connect Jerry to the music and friends from which he would forge an amazing musical phenomenon.

What was Jerry Garcia's first band?

 After Bobbie Garcia moved the family to Cazadero, north of San Francisco, primarily to get Jerry away from the teenage hoodlums he was hanging out with, Jerry started attending Analy High School in Sevastopol. The school had a big band called the Chords, and Jerry joined, struggling with his primitive guitar skills to keep up with the band's easy-listening style. Jerry would later describe the Chords' music as "businessman's bounce, high school version."

 What was Jerry's post-high school alma mater?

 The United States Army. After an incident in which he stole his mother's car, Jerry faced the alternatives that confront many wayward boys: the army, or jail. So, in 1960, 17-year-old Jerry became a soldier. If he was hoping to see the world, though, he would be disappointed: He ended up being stationed at Fort Ord near Monterey, only about 150 miles away from home.

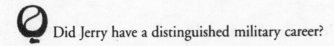

Q Did Jerry have a distinguished military career?

A Yes, but it was distinguished mostly by getting into trouble. He was written up on eight AWOLs, faced a court martial twice, and wound up being dishonorably discharged. One of the scams of which he was a part involved helping the base armorer file the serial numbers off army-issue automatic pistols so they could be sold.

Q Did Jerry get anything worthwhile out of his army experience?

A Oh, yes. His squad leader could do some finger picking on acoustic guitar. Jerry was fascinated. He smuggled an acoustic guitar onto the base and got some informal guitar lessons. Besides a new set of guitar chops, the experience introduced him to the kind of American roots music that would become the foundation of his musical career.

Q What is Phil Lesh's full name and birthday?

A Phillip Chapman Lesh was born March 15, 1940, in Berkeley, California.

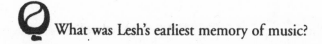

Q What was Lesh's earliest memory of music?

A Like Jerry, Phil was four years old, and his grandma played a role. His grandmother had just tuned the radio to the New York Philharmonic performing Brahms's *First Symphony.* "I walked over and sat down next to my grandmother," Lesh told journalist Hank Harrison in 1972, "and woow! This fucking thing comes out of the radio and knocks my head off. I have never been the same since."

Q What was Phil's first instrument?

A He began violin lessons when he was in third grade. But when his braces were removed at age 14, he took up the trumpet, the axe that he would play as he began to explore the world of jazz.

Q Did Phil's parents support his musical aspirations?

A They did indeed. Frank and Barbara Lesh led a typical middle-class existence, but they had refined taste in music and recognized the spark in their only child. When Phil was in high school, they moved so that he could attend Berkeley High, which had a fine music program. Phil joined the school's band, orchestra, dance band, and Pro Musica ensemble.

Q Did young Phil live up to his potential in high school?

A And how. By the time he graduated, he was putting his amazing gift for transposing keys on sight to use as he created arrangements of Stan Kenton tunes for his jazz ensemble. He went on to play second trumpet for the Oakland Symphony Orchestra and first chair in the Young People's Symphony Orchestra.

Q Where did Phil Lesh go to college?

A His musical accomplishments won him admission to San Francisco State University, but the introspective, 17-year-old loner was overwhelmed by campus life and soon dropped out. A year later, in 1958, he enrolled at the College of San Mateo, and competed for a spot on the music department's renowned jazz band. But despite his intuitive grasp of the music, he lacked the wind to play the power-jazz style the band favored, and usually ended up as second trumpet.

Q Unlike most young men of his generation, Phil Lesh never had to worry about being drafted. Why not?

A His poor eyesight rendered him unfit for military service. It wasn't for lack of trying, though; after dropping out of San Francisco State, Phil tried to enlist, hoping to join the Sixth Army Band that was stationed nearby. At the physical, a medic asked him to read the bottom line on an eye chart. "What chart?" Phil asked. "The chart on the wall." "What wall?" Thus ended his military career.

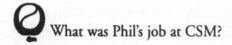
Q What was Phil's job at CSM?

A He listened to records that were returned to the college library to check for scratches and pops. It was a great way to be exposed to a tremendous range of music, and Phil felt like a kid in a candy store.

Q What was the next turn in Phil's musical path?

A In the CSM college library, he discovered the experimental journal *Music Quarterly,* and the recordings of avant garde composers like Charles Ives. The possibilities of experimental composition excited him, and he began to create unusual exercise numbers for the CSM jazz band. As Dennis McNally relates in *A Long Strange Trip,* "He would create ten-bar exercises for bizarre orchestrations like the 'mother chord,' a dissonant blast that included all twelve chromatic tones, or his first chart, in which the bass player had to tune down his instrument for the first line and then retune it for the remainder, while the brass players began in the highest register, and each section of the band was in a different key."

Q By 1962, Phil was in the music department at Mills College. What was the name of the Italian avant garde composer he studied with?

A Luciano Berio, whose groundbreaking work with electronic music in compositions like "Ommaggio a Joyce" and "Visage" would set the stage for the experimental art music to come.

Q Who was in Phil's class with Berio?

A Tom Constanten, known as T.C., who would become Phil's future roommate, song writing partner, and, briefly, keyboardist for the Grateful Dead.

Q What prophetic name was the Grateful Dead's main lyricist born with?

A Robert Hunter was born Robert Burns on June 23, 1941, and, at least for a while, shared his name with the great Scottish poet.

Q Did Robert have a stable home life?

A Scarcely. His father was an alcoholic navy man, and Robert's early years consisted of following him from base to base on the California coast. He abandoned his family when Robert was seven, and the boy ended up in a series of foster homes.

Q What was Robert's salvation during his rootless childhood?

A Books. He was a fan of Robert Louis Stevenson and Steinbeck's *The Red Pony.* Robert was also quite fond of outlaw characters like Robin Hood and Wyatt Erp. He started writing a novel when he was eleven, and managed to grind out fifty pages.

Q How did Robert acquire the last name Hunter?

A When he was eleven, his mother remarried Norman Hunter, a national sales manager for McGraw-Hill. His stepfather's intellectual presence and literary aura was the cornerstone of a stable, if somewhat conservative, home life for young Bob.

Q Which member of the original Grateful Dead was born in 1945?

A Ron McKernan, who grew up to assume the fearsome biker persona of "Pigpen." He was born on September 8 in San Bruno, California.

Q How were Pigpen's musical tastes formed?

A His father had been a boogie-woogie piano player; when Ron was born, he got a job as disk jockey with an R&B radio show. In the process, he developed a massive record collection that was heavy on blues and the wild rhythm and blues shouters of the era. His dad's record collection served as the soundtrack to Ron's childhood in a racially diverse working class neighborhood in Palo Alto, California.

Q Another founding member of the Grateful Dead was born in Palo Alto a year after Pigpen. Who was he?

A Bill Kreutzmann, who was born May 7, 1946.

Q What was Bill's first musical gig?

A Bill's mother was a dancing teacher at Stanford University.
When she noticed that her son loved to tap rhythms out on just
about any surface, she let him keep time on a tom-tom for her
dance classes.

Q Who was the youngest of the original band members?

A You need only look at any group picture ever taken of the
Grateful Dead to figure that out. Bob Weir, born October 16,
1947, was the youngster of the group.

Q Was Weir from a working class background like his band mates?

A Far from it. Bob's father trained as an engineer at Annapolis
and founded his own engineering firm; his mother ran a successful import-export business. An adopted child, Bob grew up
in the ritzy Atherton section of San Francisco, and his family
was listed in the social register.

Q How else did Bob Weir's childhood differ from those of Garcia, Lesh, and McKernan?

A He didn't grow up in a musical family. Although his mother volunteered with the symphony orchestra, it was mostly a social activity, and Bob's earliest experience with music came through his nanny, a black woman who introduced him to jazz records.

Q What childhood health problem affected Bob his entire life?

A He contracted spinal meningitis, which he credited with giving him a somewhat spacey demeanor.

Q What was Bob's first instrument?

A He took piano lessons at first; but after his piano teacher showed him how to play a little simple boogie-woogie, he irritated his parents with a constant boogie barrage, and they took the piano away. Next came a trumpet, which bothered the neighbors. Finally, his parents got him a cheap acoustic guitar as a junior high-school graduation present.

Q How did Bob do as a young scholar?

A Not well. He was a dyslexic at a time when no one knew what dyslexia was, and reading was always a struggle for him. He compensated by becoming a class clown with a talent for pranks. As a result, he bounced from school to school, including a year at a private school in Colorado that specialized in boys with behavioral problems.

Q Before Jerry Garcia, Robert Hunter, Phil Lesh, and Bob Weir were hippies, what were they?

A Beatniks. Although the Beat Generation, inaugurated in the mid-'50s with the publication of defining works like Allan Ginsberg's *Howl and Other Poems* and Jack Kerouac's *On the Road*, had largely run its artistic course by the early 1960s, the image of the "beatnik"—complete with goatee, beret, bongos, and reefers—had been indelibly imprinted on American culture. In search of personal freedom, new forms of artistic expression, and "kicks," young people flocked to the coffeehouses and small clubs looking for the scene they'd read about in Beat novels—or in the voyeuristic features on beatniks that often appeared in slick magazines like *Life* and *Look*. By one path or another, each of the founding members of the Grateful Dead were introduced to the bohemian counterculture of Palo Alto and San Francisco, and that is where they met.

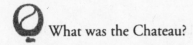

Q What was the Chateau?

A The place with the fancy sounding name was a Palo Alto rooming house near Stanford University. As Dennis McNally describes it, "The Chateau sheltered a bizarre collection of young black and white bohemian proto-artists, musicians, and weirdos, and parties there more closely resembled a Fellini film than a campus sock hop." After he was discharged from the army in January 1961, Jerry Garcia moved to Palo Alto and became part of the bohemian crowd. Jerry would flop at the Chateau on and off during his first four years in Palo Alto.

Q Jerry's indifferent attitude toward life came to an end on February 20, 1961. What happened?

A He and three friends left a party at the Chateau in search of some weed. The driver was having fun pushing the Studebaker they were in to its limits, when the car missed a curb and tumbled end over end at 90 miles an hour, ejecting Garcia and two other passengers. The third, Paul Speegle, Jerry's best friend at the time, was pinned in the car and crushed to death. Jerry escaped without serious injury, but with no way to pay for medical attention, his convalescence consisted of hanging out on a friend's couch trying to heal. Friends remember that the accident changed Jerry's attitude; while he would never become what anyone would consider disciplined, his life began to take on a single-minded focus, and that focus was music.

Q In March 1961, one of the greatest songwriting teams of rock music met for the first time. How did it happen?

A Jerry Garcia had volunteered to run stage lights for the local Commedia Dell'arte Theater's production of *Damn Yankees*. It was here that he was introduced to Robert Hunter, who had himself just finished training with the National Guard. The two ran into each other again a few days later at a coffeehouse called St. Michael's Allye that Garcia had made his virtual home, and started up a conversation. It was the beginning of a beautiful friendship.

Q An obscure, self-styled musical historian named Harry Smith made a record in 1952 that would have a profound effect on Hunter, Garcia, and many other young musicians in the 1960s. What was it?

A The *Anthology of American Folk Music*, a three-album set on Folkways Records that introduced an entire generation to styles of American roots music that might otherwise have been forgotten. Rather than rely on field recordings, as did many of the serious musicologists of the day, Smith culled his anthology from his huge collection of old 78 rpm records. At a time when music was dominated by the slick sound of post-war big band pop and the faddish, teen-oriented rock 'n' roll of Pat Boone and Ricky Nelson, the sound of the *Anthology* was a stunning revelation. Here was the music of the Carter Family, Mississippi John Hurt, Blind Lemon Jefferson, and other seminal figures of blues and country, along with hillbilly string bands, jug bands, cowboy balladeers, and gospel choirs. Garcia and his contemporaries were fascinated by the weird, funky edge of this music, and their resulting passion for roots music was the foundation for the folk music scene of the early '60s.

Q What was the first song on which Hunter and Garcia collaborated? For extra karma points, where did they write it?

A It was a folk song entitled "Black Cat," which they wrote together at one of the foci of the Palo Alto scene, Kepler's Bookstore. The two had taken to hanging out at Kepler's every day, playing guitars and singing folk songs. Their composition was a reworking of the roots music they'd been absorbing, with a hip, ironic sensibility—a formula that would stand them in good stead in years to come.

Q Did Robert and Jerry's musical collaboration ever leave the backroom at Kepler's?

A It did, for a while. The duo "Bob and Jerry" managed to snag a paying gig at a local school graduation celebration, and picked up a few sheckles playing house parties. But while they were musical soul brothers, the two were mismatched as far as their chops were concerned. Hunter was an indifferent guitarist; he really thought of himself as a writer, and had started writing a novel about the Palo Alto bohemian scene. For his part, Garcia had begun a relentless obsession with perfecting his musical skills, and wanted nothing more than to devote his life to playing music. The two continued to hang out at Kepler's, and Hunter would contribute to many of Garcia's projects over the next few years, but "Bob and Jerry" were finished as an act.

Q In Dead legend, what's the significance of the Boar's Head?

A To begin with, it was Jerry Garcia's first regular music gig. In the summer of 1961, he was invited to play at the new folk club that had just opened above a metaphysical book store between Palo Alto and San Francisco, and to bring along his friends. Payment was on a pass-the-hat basis, but the Boar's Head gigs were Jerry's first chance to collaborate with other musicians before a real audience. One of those musicians, as fate would have it, was an imposing biker-figure with a heart of gold: Ron McKernan.

Q Before he was dubbed Pigpen, Ron McKernan had two previous nicknames. What was the first?

A As a teenager, Ron was known as "Rimms," as in the rims of a spoked motorcycle wheel. It suited his image—greased-back hair, jeans, and T-shirts, a length of motorcycle chain permanently welded to his wrist. To top off the aura, he managed to get himself expelled from high school.

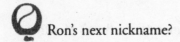

Q Ron's next nickname?

A By the time he ran into Jerry Garcia in the clubs and coffee houses of Palo Alto, he was going by handle "Blue Ron." Liberated from school, Ron took to hanging around dives in East Palo Alto, soaking up cheap wine and listening to old bluesmen like the pianist T-Bone Walker. He picked up the harmonica and acoustic guitar, and started to sit in with bands in clubs like the Boar's Head, where Garcia and Hunter had become fixtures.

Q And how did Ron come by his famous moniker?

A After a gig with Garcia, Weir, and some friends at the Boar's Head, a musician named Truck Driving Cherie Huddleston sized up Ron's aggressively grubby appearance and said, "All right for you, Pigpen." The contrast between Ron's fearsome looks and sweet demeanor made the association with the character from the *Peanuts* comic strip seem very apt, and the name stuck.

Q What did the Thunder Mountain Tub Thumpers, the Hart Valley Drifters, and the Sleepy Hollow Hog Stompers have in common?

A They were all pretty much the same guys. Throughout 1962 and 1963, Jerry, Hunter, and other roots music enthusiasts would throw together pickup groups to play clubs and parties (and once, even, a political campaign event). They'd often make up an original group name for the occasion.

Q How did Jerry Garcia meet Phil Lesh?

A By 1962, Phil was living in Berkeley, going to school, and holding down a menial job at a stock-trading firm. His chief musical outlet at the time was as a volunteer engineer at KPFA, San Francisco's groundbreaking public radio station. The station ran a program late on Saturday nights, *The Midnight Special,* that focused on acts from the burgeoning Bay Area music scene. Lesh and Garcia were traveling in the same spheres at the time— St. Michael's Alley, Kepler's Book Store, the Palo Alto Peace Center—and eventually a mutual friend who knew they were both musicians introduced them at a party in Palo Alto where Jerry was playing folk songs. Their friendship really took off a short time later, however, at another party at which Lesh was particularly impressed with Garcia's performance. They talked, and Phil conceived of getting Jerry on *The Midnight Special.* He proposed that they should go back to Phil's place in Berkeley to record a demo tape, and during the long night that followed, a 35-year partnership was born.

Q Did Jerry make it on *The Midnight Special?*

A He did indeed. In fact, the producers were so impressed by the demo tape that they took the unprecedented step of devoting an entire 90-minute show to him, spotlighting his performances and interviewing him about his music. It was the first of many appearances Jerry would make on the seminal music show over the next few years, performances that would begin to build his legend in the San Francisco music scene.

The Grateful Dead at the epicenter of the worldwide
youth movement, the corner of Haight and Ashbury.

CHAPTER TWO

Mother McCree's Uptown Jug Champions

By 1962, the country was ready for a change. America's youngest president had committed the nation to putting a man on the moon. Andy Warhol's paintings of soup cans and soap packages were turning the art world on its ear. Jazz artists like John Coltrane and Miles Davis were taking music to unimaginable new places. Black people were sick of the chains of racism, and were becoming impatient for freedom. On the radio, folk singers decried political and social evils, proclaiming that a new day was just beyond the horizon. Something was comin', just around the bend.

In San Francisco, the revolution had already begun. Young people had rejected the society of their elders and were determined to build a new one to replace it. They searched the political, artistic, and social exemplars of every time and culture, and were ready to use whatever came to hand as their building blocks—everything from Buddha to Lenin, from the cakewalk to Indian ragas, from computers to marijuana. With all that wonderful raw material, you could create almost anything: a political movement, a street theatre, a commune—or even a rock 'n' roll band.

Q With which instrument did Jerry Garcia first achieve recognition for his virtuoso chops?

A No, it wasn't the guitar. As his exploration of roots music continued into 1962, Jerry discovered the bluegrass music of legends like Bill Monroe and Flatt & Scruggs. The quick, driving, intricate sound of bluegrass banjo picking excited him, and he began to devote himself to the instrument. He quickly formed the Sleepy Hollow Hog Stompers, including Hunter on mandolin, to explore his new musical obsession.

Q "The social polarity of the time was never so clearly delineated," Phil Lesh writes in his autobiography. "The upper class drinks, the proletariat scuffles for bread." What event was he referring to?

A The marriage of Jerry Garcia and Sara Ruppenthal on April 27, 1963. The couple had met two months earlier at Kepler's Bookstore. Sara was beautiful, and well acquainted with the bohemian scene, having been a protégé of folk singer Joan Baez. She was taken by Jerry's bearded good looks, and felt a maternal instinct toward him and his friends at the Chateau. They hooked up, and Sara became pregnant. Although Sara's patrician parents tried to talk them out of it, Jerry wanted the home life he'd missed as a child, and they decided to get married. At the reception after the ceremony, Sara's family hit the bar and began drinking with a vengeance; Jerry's scruffy beatnik friends descended on the buffet line with equal ferocity.

Did Jerry's new marital status change his habits?

 Indeed it did. In an effort to be a good family man, Jerry quit hanging around his old haunts, and got a job. It was a job he was well suited for, at least—teaching guitar and banjo lessons at Dana Morgan's music store in Palo Alto. He and Sara moved into a place in the suburbs and began living some semblance of a conventional lifestyle, although Jerry's daily commute consisted of hitchhiking into Palo Alto, his instrument cases in tow.

 Jerry and Sara shared at least one evening activity that was unusual for a suburban couple. What was it?

 They formed a folk music duo and began playing in clubs, performing Carter Family tunes, old country material, and traditional songs. Sara had a good singing voice and was a versatile instrumentalist who could play guitar, banjo, mandolin, and fiddle.

 What's the next line?
When you go to Deep Ellum
Keep your money in your pants . . .

 'Cause the redheads in Deep Ellum/never give a man a chance.
"Deep Ellum Blues" was recorded by many artists since the 1930s, and was one of the numbers Jerry and Sara performed on stage. The name "Deep Ellum" referred to the Dallas red light district.

Q In 1963, Jerry got some occasional work playing in a rock 'n' roll band. What was it called? And what was his instrument?

A The manager of Dana Morgan's, Troy Weidenheimer, had a band called the Zodiacs. He invited Jerry to join them—as a bass guitar player. Troy's group wasn't keen on rehearsal and didn't know a lot of songs, so their gigs often consisted of long jam sessions. Jerry felt a bit out of place playing rock on the bass, but he loved the loose, fun atmosphere the Zodiacs created.

Q Weidenheimer played electric guitar with the Zodiacs; Jerry played bass. Who was on drums and harmonica?

A Bill Kreutzmann was the drummer; Ron McKernan blew harp. Three of the five founding members of the Grateful Dead had found one another.

Q The 1963 Monterey Folk Festival featured big acts like Bob Dylan and Peter, Paul, and Mary. In the amateur division, an obscure bluegrass act won the competition for Best Group. Who were they?

A The Hart Valley Drifters, fronted by Jerry Garcia, who also won the Best Banjo Player award. The Drifters also featured Robert Hunter on bass fiddle.

Q Was Jerry a big Dylan fan?

A No, at least not yet. Dylan had moved on from his early image as a Woody Guthrie imitator singing established folk material, and began writing original numbers, like "Blowin' in the Wind," "Masters of War," and "Don't Think Twice," that would establish him as one of the era's great songwriters. Sharing the attitude of many folk music purists at the time, Jerry believed in trying to replicate the sound of traditional music, and distained Dylan's attempts to innovate.

Q On December 31, 1963, Jerry was hanging out at his practice room at Dana Morgan's, waiting for students to arrive. Probably because it was New Year's Eve, none of them showed up. Who did?

A Bob Weir, and two of his friends. The sixteen-year-old Weir was attracted by the sound of Jerry's banjo; he and his friends went in and started chatting with Garcia, who opened the front of the store so the group could select instruments and start a jam session.

Q Bob and his friends would soon put their own group together. What were they called?

A The Uncalled Four. Playing at the occasional hootenanny, they performed a mix of songs by popular folk acts like Joan Baez and the Kingston Trio.

Q In 1964, Jerry decided to take a break from the rigors of blue-grass music and got together a new group. What kind of music did they play?

A Jug music. Named after one of the principal bass instruments they featured, jug bands played loose, loopy, bluesy dance tunes for black audiences in the South in the 1920s and '30s. A few of them, such as Shade's Memphis Jug Band and Cannon's Jug Stompers, were popular enough to make records; both bands were featured on the *Anthology of American Folk Music*, which introduced the genre to a new generation. Bay Area musician Jim Kweskin put together a jug band act he named after himself, and their album and performances were popular in Berkeley. With its funny, racy songs and low-brow instruments like the washboard and the kazoo, jug music was just for fun—unlike the hyper-seriousness that pervaded the rest of the folk scene.

Q What was Jerry's jug band named?

A Mother McCree's Uptown Jug Champions.

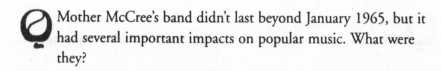

Q Mother McCree's band didn't last beyond January 1965, but it had several important impacts on popular music. What were they?

A To begin with, the band featured Garcia on guitar, Bob Weir on washtub bass and jug, and Pigpen on harmonica; the three would become the core of the Grateful Dead. Several of the jug band numbers they played, like "Viola Lee Blues," "Minglewood Blues," and "Beat It on Down the Line," would be transformed to become part of the Dead's repertoire. In fact, when Pigpen suggested that the jug band music could easily be electrified (in the manner of the new British Invasion band, the Rolling Stones), he convinced Jerry that rock 'n' roll might in fact be worth pursuing full-time.

Q What was Jerry Garcia's last homage to bluegrass?

A The summer of 1964 would become legendary as Freedom Summer, as young people headed to the South to challenge segregation by violating Jim Crow, forcibly integrating lunch stands and public buses. Jerry Garcia and his friend Sandy Rothman headed south too; but rather than spreading liberation, they went to soak up the sounds of their beloved bluegrass music at its source. They stopped first in Los Angeles to pick up the members of a bluegrass band called the Kentucky Colonels; the little caravan spent the summer traveling throughout the Midwest and Southern states.

Q What bluegrass legend did the boys meet on their excursion?

A The highlight of the trip was a stop at Bean Blossom, Indiana, at Bill Monroe's Brown County Jamboree, where the group had a tongue-tied meeting with the Father of Bluegrass himself.

Q Like most folk purists, Jerry Garcia and his friends thought that the rock 'n' roll music of the early 1960s was trash, a commodity for teenagers. What happened to change their minds?

A Two things. First was the Rolling Stones. Mick Jagger and Keith Richards had been part of England's blues craze, and were now having a great deal of success with bouncy, electrified versions of music by American blues icons like Muddy Waters and Howlin' Wolf. It was music with which the San Francisco folkies were quite familiar, and it set the Stones apart from the slick, cheerful records the Beatles had made.

The second happening was the release of the Beatles' film, *A Hard Day's Night.* Beatlemania was sweeping the planet, and the group could have simply thrown together an easy piece of movie fluff to cash in on their fame, as Elvis Presley had been doing. Instead, they worked with genius director Richard Lester to create a cheekily-ironic comedy that used their smart, iconoclastic sense of humor and style to great effect. Suddenly, rock was something cool for grown-ups, too.

What was Phil Lesh's reaction to seeing *A Hard Day's Night?*

 He went home, combed his hair forward over his forehead, and cut his bangs, creating his own version of the Beatle haircut. His roommates thought he was daft, and his hairstyle got him in trouble with his employer at the time, the U.S. Postal Service.

 What lesson did Jerry Garcia draw from *A Hard Day's Night?*

 Years later, he recalled the message the film had for him: "You can be young, you can be far-out, and you can still make it." The lighthearted, arty, madcap spirit of the Beatles appealed to him, and made the notion of playing rock 'n' roll more attractive.

 Among the proto-Dead members, whose idea was it to start an electric band?

 Pigpen's. The blues had always been his first love, and he'd heard electric blues bands in the dives of East Palo Alto for years. When the Rolling Stones came on the scene, Pigpen knew his blues chops were just as good as any Englishman's, and he started pressing Garcia with the idea that they should start an electrified blues band. By late 1964, the craze for amplified instruments had hit them: Bob Weir, entranced by the Beatles, had taken up electric rhythm guitar, and Pigpen had started teaching himself Farfisa organ. Garcia started to take the idea seriously.

Q So they had two guitars, an organ, and Dana Morgan's son, Dana Jr., on bass guitar. They needed a drummer. Who did they get?

A Bill Kreutzmann, with whom Jerry and Pigpen had previously played in the Zodiacs. One of the most proficient drummers in the Bay Area music scene, Bill had been gigging with an R&B band called the Legends, fronted by a black singer and sporting the requisite matching flashy suits. Jerry asked him to join his new band and he was, Jerry would later report, "delighted."

Q What was Bill Kreutzmann's day job at the time?

A He was a salesman at a wig shop, a job he got to support his wife and daughter in their tiny Palo Alto apartment. He also picked up extra funds giving drum lessons at Dana Morgan's.

Q What was the name of the first band to feature Jerry Garcia, Bob Weir, Ron "Pigpen" McKernan, and Bill Kreutzmann playing rock music on electric instruments? And what inspired the name?

A Bob Weir was reading J.R.R. Tolkien's *Lord of the Rings* trilogy, and the spirit of magic was in the air. Weir, Pigpen, and Garcia came up with the name, "The Warlocks."

What was the Warlocks' first gig?

 Their first public performances were at a Menlo Park restaurant, Magoo's Pizza Parlor. It was a strange place for a rock band; the quarters were cramped, and the place didn't have a permit for dancing. But the band members invited their friends from the Palo Alto scene and the gigs turned out to be a rousing success.

 Who was among the audience at the Warlocks' second appearance at Magoo's?

 Phil Lesh, who grooved to the sound of "the loudest music I had ever heard." As the Warlocks swung into the blues classic they'd picked up from a Rolling Stones record, "I'm a King Bee," Lesh later recalled, "When Pig came in with the vocal, I had to look away; it was just so sexual—the sound of his voice over the mike delivering slithery insinuations and promises of pleasures beyond comprehension—and when he took a harp lead (backed by Jerry in call-and-response pattern), it absolutely ate my mind."

Q The Warlocks were beginning to take off, but they had a problem. What was this perennial plague of garage bands everywhere?

A Their bass player sucked. Having the son of a music store owner in the band had several advantages, including access to electric instruments, but Dana Jr. just couldn't cut it as a rock bass guitarist; his understanding of the most basic music theory needed to jam with three-chord rock songs was severely limited, and the other band members had to coach him constantly on what notes to play.

Q How did they solve their bass player problem?

A Garcia remembered that Phil Lesh had expressed an interest in the bass guitar, and invited him to join the Warlocks.

Q How much experience had Phil had playing bass when he was asked to join the Warlocks?

A Zero; he'd never even held one before. With his highly developed musicianship, however, he knew he could master it quickly, and he agreed to join the band on bass if Jerry would give him a quick lesson. After the Warlocks' gig that night, they went back to Jerry's house and Garcia demonstrated the basic scales on the top strings of a guitar. Phil borrowed a standard guitar from a friend and started practicing. "I didn't know if this trip would last more than a week," Phil would recall in his autobiography. "I was going to give it all I had while it lasted."

Q Like a lot of small-time rock bands, the Warlocks played mostly covers, with very little original material. What's significant about the band's repertoire?

A A number of the songs that were regulars at the Warlocks' gigs—"King Bee," "Little Red Rooster," "Promised Land," Dylan's "It's All Over Now, Baby Blue," "Johnny B. Goode"— would become Grateful Dead standards, revisited over and over at thousands of concerts over the next 30 years.

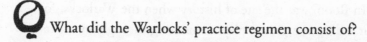

Q What did the Warlocks' practice regimen consist of?

A They sequestered themselves in the rehearsal room at Guitars Unlimited in Menlo Park (where Jerry and Bob had gotten jobs teaching guitar lessons), and played the same handful of songs, over and over, often all day long. Lesh wasn't the only one just learning his instrument; even the guitar players were still getting used to electric instruments, and then there was the need to expand their limited repertoire of songs. Vocal harmonies were also something they needed to work on; none of them were particularly strong vocalists, and Lesh had never sang and played at the same time before (tough to do on the trumpet). The obsessive rehearsal paid off, though, and soon they had mastered the basics and were ready to explore new territory.

Q Magoo's Pizza Parlor didn't last long as a live music venue: despite the lack of a city permit, customers refused to stop dancing. What was the Warlocks' next regular gig?

A After short stints at clubs like the Fireside, Big Al's, and the Cinnamon A-Go-Go, they finally became the house band at a place called the In Room in Belmont, where they played six nights a week to an audience that combined suburban lounge drinkers with some of the freakier elements of the Palo Alto scene.

Q The In Room was the site of history when the Warlocks, for the first time as a group, played one song through an entire 45-minute set. What was the number?

A Wilson Pickett's "In the Midnight Hour." As the Zodiacs had done previously, the Warlocks had been extending their limited repertoire with long solos; when the rhythm section got bored repeating the same backup, Lesh and Kreutzmann would begin improvising variations as well. Lesh, who saw the similarity with the improvisational composition techniques of jazz, began encouraging his band mates to listen to the bop music of John Coltrane. The band began experimenting with long, sponta-neous reinventions of the blues, R&B, and jug band songs they knew how to play.

Q The Warlocks themselves thought they might be inventing a new art form. What did the management of the In Room think about it?

A The strange, stunningly loud music they played and the even-stranger people the Warlocks attracted were not quite what the suburban lounge was looking for in a bar band, and they were eventually canned. As they packed up their gear after the last show, the In Room's manager pronounced his verdict on them: "You guys will never make it. You're too weird."

Q Was the next Warlocks gig a step in the direction of musical fame?

A 'Fraid not. The next, and, as it turned out, last club gig for the Warlocks was as backup to the strippers at a San Francisco dive called Pierre's.

Q When the Warlocks weren't practicing or performing, how did they like to spend their time?

A Getting high on a relatively new drug that was beginning to become quite popular with the San Francisco bohemian set: LSD.

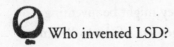

Who invented LSD?

Swiss chemist Albert Hoffman. In 1943, Hoffman was working for the pharmaceutical manufacturer Sandoz Laboratories, trying to develop drugs from various medicinal plants. He was trying to synthesize lysergic acid, the chemical in argot fungus that caused the medieval hallucinatory condition known as argotism. On his twenty-fifth attempt, he touched his mouth with his fingers, accidentally ingesting the drug. Feeling ill, he went home, and tripped for the next two hours. Three days later, he intentionally took 250 micrograms—and while riding his bike home from the laboratory, he watched the world disintegrate and recreate itself in colorful visions. Thus was lysergic acid diethylamide 25, LSD for short, introduced to this astral plane.

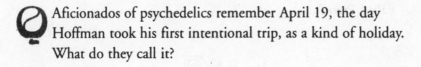

Aficionados of psychedelics remember April 19, the day Hoffman took his first intentional trip, as a kind of holiday. What do they call it?

"Bicycle Day."

Q Hoffman went on to explore mescaline, psilocybin, and a number of other hallucinogenic drugs, publishing enthusiastic reports of their effects. Did all that heavy drug use ruin his life?

A Um, no. As of this writing, he is still going strong, well past age 100, and still giving the occasional speech about the chemical he discovered. But while Hoffman believed that hallucinogens could be important tools in psychoanalysis and other forms of self-discovery, he was horrified to see LSD become a party drug, and feared the damage that acid might be capable of in casual use.

Q Who was ultimately responsible for turning the Dead on to acid?

A The Central Intelligence Agency. In the early 1960s, the CIA's now-notorious MK-ULTRA project was running a variety of investigations into what they referred to as "psychotomimetic" drugs such as LSD, psilocybin, and mescaline. The Agency was hoping these drugs could be used as some kind of truth serum in interrogations, or at least to drive people insane when they needed to. They were in for a shock: many of the people who took psychedelics in these testing sessions not only didn't go crazy, they seemed to enjoy the experience.

Q Which member of the Dead's inner circle was involved in the MK-ULTRA experiments?

A One of the testing programs was run out of the Veterans Administration Hospital in Menlo Park; among the paid test subjects was Robert Hunter. Hunter shared his Joycean session notes with excited friends like Jerry Garcia, who said, "God, I've got to have some of that."

Q What was Phil Lesh's first experience with LSD?

A In the winter of 1964, a coworker dropped a foil-wrapped sugar cube in his hand and whispered "Here ya go. Two hundred and fifty mikes." It was a moment Lesh was prepared for; rumors had been circulating about the marvelous effects of hallucinogens, and Phil had been reading such classic books on the subject as Aldous Huxley's *The Doors of Perception* and Alan Watt's *The Joyous Cosmology.* He knew that 250 micrograms of acid was a big hit, so he split it with roommate and future songwriting partner Tom Constanten. In his autobiography, Phil recalled the experience after downing his half: "I don't remember much after that, just a kaleidoscope of emotional peaks; at one point I found myself outside in the front yard on a beautiful starry night, conducting, with extravagant gestures, Mahler's great *Tragic Symphony,* which was blasting from the house. . . My guess is that I'd left more than half the dose behind in T.C.'s portion; judging from the expression on his face as I walked in the door the day he did his share, his experience was somewhat more ecstatic than mine had been."

Q And when did Mr. Garcia first bend his mind?

A April 1965. Jerry got two hits of LSD as a reward for helping a friend move, and took one home to his wife Sara. Jerry had a great trip, "a perfectly wonderful time," as he would later recall. Sara had a harder time of it: after some extended mirror-gazing led to an incipient freak-out, she walked over to the home of the CIA-acid veteran, Robert Hunter, who helped talk her down.

Q Did the Warlocks ever cut a record?

A Indeed they did. On November 3, 1965, the band was auditioned by Autumn Records at Golden State Recorders, a cheap studio by the train station near Market Street. The demo recorded original tunes like "Caution (Do Not Cross Tracks)," "Mindbender," and "Can't Come Down," along with Gordon Lightfoot's "In the Early Morning Rain."

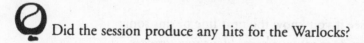

Q Did the session produce any hits for the Warlocks?

A The Autumn Records folks were not impressed, and the recordings remained unreleased until the arrival of the Grateful Dead anthologies *So Many Roads* (1999) and *The Golden Road* (2001). But the tapes did circulate and graced the airwaves of Berkeley's alternative FM radio scene.

Q Identify the song:
Well someone trying to tell me where it's at
And how I do this and why I do that
With secret smiles like a Cheshire cat
And leather wings like a vampire bat...

A "Can't Come Down," written by Jerry Garcia in 1965.
It was one of the Dead's first numbers, but they stopped
performing it in concert after 1966. It later appeared on
the *So Many Roads* anthology.

Q What's the next line?
The friendly stranger called my name
He only wants me for his game
But it don't matter, just the same . . .

A *I'll bend his mind.* Jerry Garcia and Phil Lesh collaborated on
this song, "Mindbender," in 1965, and it was one of the songs
the Warlocks recorded as a demo. The Dead only performed
the song live twice, in 1966.

Q Let's see if you know the next line of this song:
Oh I come to you as a ragged laughing stranger
And you come to me an angel of the night
So I'll dance and we will sing, for it doesn't mean a thing . . .

A *To remember that the only time is now.* Another song from the
Golden State Recorders demo session in 1965; the only docu-
mented live performance of Jerry Garcia's "The Only Time is
Now" was at the Matrix Theatre in San Francisco in 1966.

Q What's the next line?
Lay down last night, Lord, I could not take my rest
Lay down last night, Lord, I could not take my rest . . .

R *My mind was wandering like the wild geese in the West.*
The Dead's version of the traditional song, "I Know You Rider,"
was one of the earliest numbers in their repertoire and one of
the first they recorded; but unlike many of their other early
numbers, they returned to this song again and again over the
next three decades, often pairing it in concert with "China Cat
Sunflower."

Q Shortly after that abortive recording session, the Warlocks were
no more. What happened?

R While browsing in a record store bin, Phil Lesh discovered a
single by another band calling themselves the Warlocks. The
Garcia-Lesh-Weir-McKernan-Kreutzmann collective needed a
new name.

Q Whatever became of the Warlocks who made the record Phil
found?

R No one is sure who they were. But it could have been the
Warlocks from New York featuring Lou Reed, which later
became the Velvet Underground. Or it might have been the
Texas band of that name, the guitarists of which went on to
form ZZ Top.

Q What did the Vikings, His Own Sweet Advocates, and the Mythical Ethical Icicle Tricycle have in common?

A They were all band names proposed by various members of the Warlocks, and ultimately rejected. Bill wanted a name that sounded like a black R&B band; Bob's contribution was a spin on "devil's advocate," and Jerry contributed the tripped-out wordplay. They weren't quite sure what they wanted, but with the rise of San Francisco bands with names like the Charlatans, the Great Society, and the Jefferson Airplane, they knew they needed something weird and fun.

Q How did the 1956 edition of *Funk and Wagnall's New Practical Standard Dictionary* change the history of American popular music?

A The ex-Warlocks had been brainstorming for a new name, paging through reference works like Bartlett's *Quotations*, but nothing clicked. Finally, after smoking the hallucinogenic drug DMT, Jerry opened a copy of Funk and Wagnall's. "Everything else on the page went blank, diffuse, just sort of oozed away," Garcia recalled, "and there was GRATEFUL DEAD, big black letters edged all around in gold, man." Lesh loved it; Weir thought it was too morbid. But Jerry was hooked, and from that moment on, the Warlocks became known as the Grateful Dead.

What, exactly, are the grateful dead?

 The term describes a recurring character in folk stories and ballads. In the typical tale, the hero comes upon a corpse that has not been laid to rest as punishment for some offense. The hero of the tale rights the wrong, allowing the corpse to receive a decent burial. Later, in the midst of some daunting challenge, the hero is aided by a mysterious companion—it turns out to have been the ghost of the now-interred dead, grateful for services rendered.

Hanging out on the porch of their headquarters at 710 Ashbury Street.

CHAPTER THREE

The Rainbow Explodes

Who'd have guessed? A chemical developed to treat migraines and tested as an insanity pill would soon inspire thousands to drop out of straight society and devote themselves to spiritual and artistic discovery. A fad variety of rhythm 'n' blues, heretofore the province of teenage novelty records, would be transformed into a powerful force of cultural change. And who would have guessed that these two elements would combine to create a scene that would shake American society to its core?

From this primal mixture of acid, music, and love was born the San Francisco Sound, as bands like the Jefferson Airplane, Quicksilver Messenger Service, and Big Brother and the Holding Company combined rock with influences from jazz, soul, and even Indian classical music to create "dem ol' cozmic blues." In the aging ballrooms left over from their parents' swing dances, kids in bizzare costumes gathered in the pulsing lights and wildly amplified sound to share a communal trip to the center of the mind.

If Jerry Garcia, Bob Weir, Phil Lesh, Ron McKernan, and Bill Kreutzmann hadn't been there as a musical spark that helped ignite the incandescent youth culture of the 1960s and '70s, it probably would have happened one way or another. There may still have been girls in day-glo paisley headbands and boys with shoulder-length hair. But they wouldn't have been hitchhiking to California looking for the love-in. The Grateful Dead's gently fatalistic good humor, their enthusiasm for musical innovation, their love of American roots music, and their quintessentially laid-back approach to life set the tone for the soft explosion that was on the way, the vibrations of which reverberate to this day.

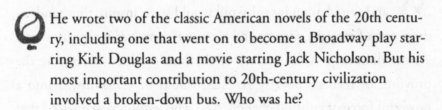

Q He wrote two of the classic American novels of the 20th century, including one that went on to become a Broadway play starring Kirk Douglas and a movie starring Jack Nicholson. But his most important contribution to 20th-century civilization involved a broken-down bus. Who was he?

A Kenneth Elton Kesey, born September 17, 1935, in La Junta, California. A popular jock and drama club kid in high school, Ken Kesey took up writing at Stanford. There he met other writers and artists who were fascinated by beat culture, and joined in forming a bohemian enclave on Perry Lane in Palo Alto. In 1960, he was one of the volunteer test subjects to be dosed with psychedelic drugs at the Veterans Administration Hospital in Menlo Park, and smuggled samples of the drugs to his friends at Perry Lane. While working as an orderly at the same VA hospital, Kesey came up with the idea for his best-known work, *One Flew Over the Cuckoo's Nest,* the story of the rebellious Randle P. McMurphy's struggle against the tyrannical Nurse Ratched. With the money he earned from the success of the book, Kesey set up house in La Honda, which became the scene of endless acid-fueled parties. Kesey believed LSD was destined to liberate mankind, and that evangelistic spirit led him and a band of followers to paint a bus in psychedelic colors, pack it full of film and sound equipment, and take it on the road in 1964.

Q What name did Kesey's psychedelic tribe adopt?

A They called themselves the Merry Pranksters.

Q Oh yeah, the bus. To establish yourself as a fully-credentialed freak, state the bus's name, its make and year, and its final resting place.

A The name, painted up where the destination is usually found, was Further. The bus was a 1939 International Harvester. And if you answered the last question "The Smithsonian Institute," you're a victim of a prank—the one in the Smithsonian is a copy. The real Further is permanently parked and rusting away on Ken Kesey's farm near Eugene, Oregon.

Q Where might you have read about the Merry Pranksters and their scene?

A New Journalism pioneer Tom Wolfe's book about Kesey and company, *The Electric Kool-Aid Acid Test*, became a perennial best-seller.

Q Who was the first member of the Grateful Dead to encounter Kesey?

A Phil Lesh. Back in 1959, while going to school at the College of San Mateo, Phil discovered the Palo Alto beatnik scene. A big part of that scene was Perry Lane in Menlo Park, and Phil started hanging out every weekend at the home of Vic Lowell, a Stanford assistant professor who hosted a continuous party. When the music got too loud, Vic's next-door neighbor—Kesey—would come over to throw everybody out.

Q What did Allan Ginsberg, Ram Dass, Hunter S. Thompson, and the Hells Angels have in common?

A They were all part of the party scene at Ken Kesey's place. It was Thompson, the gonzo journalist who had just finished his book on the Hells Angels, who introduced the motorcycle club members to Kesey's crowd. Although the Angels would never prefer acid to beer, the San Francisco set saw them as true individualists, and the outlaw band with a taste for Harley Davidsons and occasional violence eventually became part of hippy culture.

Q What historic event occurred on November 27, 1965, in Soquel, California?

A The Grateful Dead dropped acid with Ken Kesey. Phil Lesh's friend, Page Browning, was part of the Pranksters' scene, and managed to get them invited to the very first Acid Test. Unlike the expansive ballroom events that would soon come, the test was in a private home, and there was no live music. But there were the projectors, lighting and sound equipment, and of course a lot of people taking LSD. The Dead members had a great time and got along well with Kesey; a few days later they drove to his place in La Honda to talk, and it was agreed that the band would play at the next Acid Test.

Q How did that gig go?

A Well, there were some problems. First was the crowd: this was the first event for which the famous posters with the slogan "Can YOU Pass the Acid Test?" were used for publicity, and they worked—a big crowd showed up for the second test. But the venue was another private home, and with the band set up on one side of the house, the Pranksters' equipment on the other, and a few hundred stoned people crammed in between, the effect was, as Lesh later recalled, "a mind-numbing blur of noise, light, and heat."

Q History was made again just a few days later. What was special about the gig the Grateful Dead played on December 10, 1965?

A It was the first show produced by Bill Graham at the Fillmore Auditorium. A German Jew who had escaped the Holocaust as a child, the 34-year-old Graham had held a number of jobs, including a stint as a singing waiter. His interest in acting led him to join the Mime Troupe, an in-your-face street theatre group that performed politically charged material in public parks. When one of the Mime Troupe members was arrested for public indecency during a performance, Graham orchestrated a variety of events to elicit public outrage and support. These included a series of fundraising benefit concerts; after the first was a big success, Graham knew he needed a larger venue and chose a down-at-heels ballroom. The Fillmore, and later incarnations like the Fillmore West and the Fillmore East in New York, became the scene of some of the most famous concerts in pop music history, including acts like the Jefferson Airplane, Quicksilver Messenger Service, Janis Joplin, Jimi Hendrix, and, of course, the Grateful Dead.

Q Where was the original Fillmore located?

A On the second floor of a building on the corner of Fillmore and Geary in San Francisco.

What else was historic about that first Fillmore show?

 It was the first time the ex-Warlocks performed publicly as the Grateful Dead. Graham hated the new name, and resisted putting it on an easel listing the acts; he compromised with the band by co-billing them as "Formerly the Warlocks."

 What did the third Acid Test have that the first two did not?

 By the third test, held on Saturday, December 11, all the elements that people remember the Acid Tests for were in place. The first was a real hall, the Big Beat Club in Palo Alto. The second was a band called the Grateful Dead, set up on the other end of the hall from the Merry Pranksters' conglomeration of light and sound machines, both collectives cranking away simultaneously. And the third element was the big bucket of acid-spiked Kool-Aid that was the source of the communal trip. These came together to create a space in which the audience was the real show, in which people with many backgrounds and interests could gather to seek personal awareness, engage in creative experimentation, and experience the group mind. As Jerry Garcia told *Rolling Stone* in 1970, "The Acid Test was the prototype for our whole basic trip . . . It was something more incredible than just rock & roll and a light show; it was just a million times more incredible."

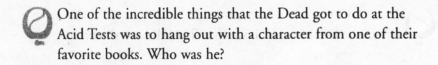

Q One of the incredible things that the Dead got to do at the Acid Tests was to hang out with a character from one of their favorite books. Who was he?

A Neal Cassady, the chief muse of the Beat Generation. He was the prototype for Dean Moriarty, the hero of Jack Kerouac's *On the Road,* a novel that was (and still is) required reading for hip kids. He also appears in the first Beat novel, John Clellon Holmes's *Go,* and Allen Ginsberg dedicated *Howl* to him. Born in 1926 in Denver in the back seat of a jalopy, Cassady was raised in a series of reform schools and juvenile prisons, and grew up to live the life of a hobo. Blowing into New York in the late 1940s, he met Kerouac, Ginsberg, and William Burroughs, who would go on to pen *Naked Lunch.* Their experiments with pot, amphetamines, and freedom became the foundation of the Beat Movement; Cassady's later involvement with the Pranksters marked an important link between the bohemian culture of the '50s and the youth culture of the '60s.

Q What three personal attributes is Neal Cassady remembered for?

A There were his good looks: his muscular body, chiseled facial features, and piercing blue eyes remained striking all his life. Then there was his approach to conversation: a brilliant, mercurial, and mile-a-minute talker, Cassady could carry on multiple conversations on widely diverse topics simultaneously, often seeming to intuit what you were about to say. And there was his driving, remembered by Kerouac in *On the Road* and by everyone who was ever his passenger. He drove fast and with an apparent recklessness that was punctuated by moments of amazing extrasensory perception in which he could find traffic holes where none existed and react to hazards before they appeared.

Q Besides the cross-country odyssey in *On the Road*, what was Neal's claim to driving fame?

A Next to the road trip in Kerouac's novel, Cassady is best remembered as the pilot of the Merry Prankster bus, Further.

Q People who saw Neal Cassady at the Acid Tests also remember his juggling skills. What item did he juggle?

A A small sledge hammer, which he would toss, flip, and catch unerringly, despite appearing not to pay attention to what he was doing.

Q Cassady gets a mention in one of the Dead's most important early compositions. Quote the lines.

A In the middle section of "The Other One," a bus stop magically appears:
The bus came by and I got on
That's when it all began
There was cowboy Neal at the wheel
Of a bus to never-never land...

Q LSD, freaky lights, and audience participation weren't the only parts of the Dead legend that got started at the Acid Tests. Name another.

A The practice of taping virtually every live Grateful Dead performance began at the tests as well. As they had during their 1964 bus expedition, the Pranksters were in the habit of filming and audiotaping just about everything they did. It was a habit the Dead would acquire as well, and later encourage their fans to engage in. As a result, we can follow the performing career of the Grateful Dead from their earliest days to their final shows, thanks to thousands of tapes in the band's "vault."

Q When the Grateful Dead played at the Acid Tests, Pigpen ended up doing most of the lead vocals. Why?

A He was the only member of the band who wasn't too high to sing. While the other band members had been doing LSD regularly for some months, the Acid Tests were the first time they had ever performed while tripping. Garcia, Lesh, and Weir felt that the chemical enhancement helped them push the music beyond its boundaries, but it did create some challenges—like timing the dose so that they could get their equipment set up before they were too far beyond the doors of perception. Pigpen, however, was more of a cheap wine kind of guy, and was usually one of the few people at an Acid Test who wasn't on acid.

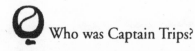

Q Who was Captain Trips?

A It was Jerry Garcia's nickname at the Acid Tests.

Q The band encountered another figure at the tests who would become an important part of their inner circle, although he first came to their attention while having a very noisy freakout. Who was he?

A Augustus Owsley Stanley III, known to his friends, and eventually to Deadheads everywhere, simply as "Bear." The son of an aristocratic Kentucky family, Bear was a misfit genius whose abortive attempt at an engineering career resulted in short stints at Rocketdyne and the Jet Propulsion Laboratory before he dropped out and discovered hallucinogens in the early 1960s. After trying genuine Sandoz acid, Stanley wanted a steady supply of good LSD, and in those days there were only two ways to get it: go to work for the CIA, or learn to make it yourself. Bear chose the latter option, and began producing hits that became legendary for their strength and purity. He was also an audio buff, and his state-of-the-art hi-fi equipment became the Dead's first sound system.

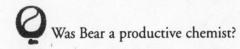

Q Was Bear a productive chemist?

A It's estimated that between 1965 and 1967, he produced 450 grams of high-grade crystalline LSD—enough for more than a million acid hits, about half of which he gave away for free. It was his product that fueled the Acid Tests and the tripped-out San Francisco counterculture that soon followed them.

Q What about the freakout?

A It happened during an Acid Test at Muir Beach, north of San Francisco. To Bear, it sounded like Jerry Garcia's guitar was emitting piercing, high-frequency shrieks; he later reported that Jerry's instrument "seemed to come out of the universe and try to eat me alive." He responded by pushing a chair across the wooden floor, creating his own high-pitched racket.

Q In January, the Merry Prankster's Acid Tests in the San Francisco area came to an abrupt end. What happened?

A Ken Kesey was busted for pot twice in short order. Wanting to stay out of jail, he faked his own death in an auto crash and headed for Mexico. The Pranksters moved their base of operations to Los Angeles to be closer to him, and Kesey made regular forays across the border to attend their LA events until the police finally caught him. He spent five months in prison, and afterward bought a farm in Oregon and moved out of California for good.

Q What was the Pink House?

A A pink stucco place off Western Avenue in Los Angeles on the edge of the section known as Watts. Located next to a whorehouse, it was the place where the Dead spent three months in 1966, trying to break into the big-time music business and living off Bear's money.

Q What was the principal element in the Dead's diet during their sojourn in Los Angeles?

A Steak. Bear had an idea that meat was the most cost-effective source of nutrition, and that was all he ate. Since Bear was buying the groceries, that's what the band ate too, sawing steaks off a side of beef in the refrigerator.

Q And did they succeed in getting their big break in the music industry?

A No, which was hardly surprising, considering they knew nothing about the record companies and had no contacts of any kind in the LA music scene. They collaborated with the Pranksters on a few Acid Tests, none of which were particularly successful; their vibe had not, apparently, followed them from the Bay Area. In fact, at an Acid Test in Watts, an extremely potent batch of Kool-Aid and a raid by the LAPD combined to create a bum trip of legendary proportions.

Q That Watts Acid Test contributed a particularly daffy, but enduring, tidbit to American popular culture. What was it?

A One of the Pranksters who was arrested that night (although LSD was not, at the time, illegal) was Paul Foster, who had his face painted half black and half silver. Foster's makeup was the inspiration for the famous "Blue Boy" episode of the television series *Dragnet*, in which LAPD detectives Friday and Gannon have their first encounter with someone on LSD. "The story you are about to see is true . . ."

Q Did the Dead get anything at all of value from their time in LA?

A New management. Bear invited Rock Scully, who had been the manager of the Charlatans, and his partner, Danny Rifkin, to assume the band's management. Neither had much experience in the music business; but managing a band like the Dead, whose primary employment was free benefit concerts and pass-the-hat parties, gave them the chance to start slow. It was a lasting arrangement, and both individuals would be part of the Grateful Dead family until the 1990s.

Q By March 1966, the Dead had had enough of Los Angeles, and wanted to return to the Bay Area—but there was a problem. What prevented their return, and how did they overcome the challenge?

A They were broke. In an attempt to generate some cash, Bear took the rest of his stash of crystalline acid and created doses by rubbing it into titrate boards. The resultant product was dubbed Blue Cheer, and it was the only thing they did in Los Angeles that was a financial success—Bear sold it immediately. Finally, Rock Scully managed to secure the band a gig at the Longshoreman's Hall in San Francisco that would pay enough to finance the trip. The band climbed into their dilapidated cars and beat it on down the road back home.

Q Upon their return, the band needed someplace to live, and they found a place that seemed like paradise. What was it called?

A Olompali, once a village of the Miwok tribe, near the bay in Marin County north of San Francisco. In a setting framed by mountains, oak forests, and the Pacific Ocean, they got a great rental deal on a big adobe house that even had a swimming pool. It was a beautiful, secluded retreat, ideal for loud music and uninhibited partying, and all in all a dramatic and welcome contrast from the squalor in Watts.

Q Grateful Graduate Deadhead Level Question: What does "Olompali" mean in the Miwok language?

A Roughly translated, "village of the southern people."

Q In the early summer of 1966, the Dead threw a housewarming party to introduce their San Francisco-area friends to Olompali. Can you name some of the luminaries who attended?

A There were the members of the Jefferson Airplane, including lead guitarist Jorma Kaukonen, who'd been Jerry's friend since their folkie days. Grace Slick, who at the time was singing with the Great Society, showed up; but she wasn't fond of parties or of LSD, so she left early. Janis Joplin, another acquaintance of the folk scene who had taken up rock as lead singer of Big Brother and the Holding Company, was lounging next to the pool, which was full of frolicking naked women. And the ubiquitous Neal Cassady brought his hammer. As Kaukonen recalled the party, "It was rock star heaven."

Q While the Dead were in LA, there had been a significant change in the San Francisco music scene. What was it?

A The era of the rock ballroom had begun. Bill Graham had purchased the Fillmore and was staging shows there every weekend; a psychedelic art collective called the Family Dog was doing the same thing at the old Avalon Ballroom at Sutter and Van Ness Avenue. The ballrooms offered the same kind of scene as the Acid Tests had—light shows, live dance music, and a big floor where people could do pretty much whatever they wanted. But instead of being sporadic, impromptu events, held as benefits or just for the fun of it, ballroom shows were regular and dependable—and generated profits for the ballroom owners. In any event, the scene was ready-made for the Grateful Dead, who became ballroom regulars just as soon as they returned.

Q Identify the song:
I said look, look, look at me
I said what, what, what do you see
You see a broken heart
My baby's 'bout to set me free...

A A live recording of Pigpen's "You See a Broken Heart," sung by Bob Weir, was made in March 1966 and released 44 years later on the *Rare Cuts and Oddities 1966* collection (2001). It's another number that didn't stay in the Dead's repertoire long.

Q The July 2, 1966, edition of the *Saturday Evening Post* introduced a new word to the American national lexicon. What was it?

A Hippie. The San Francisco newspapers had been using the term, a semi-derisive derivative of "hipster," to describe the young seekers of art, drugs, music, and freedom who had begun to flock to the city. Though the *Post* didn't get the spelling right, its article "Daddy is a Hippy" was probably the first national use of the word.

Q When the band got back from LA, Scully and Rifkin set up an office in a neighborhood that would become legendary. Where did they go? And for extra love beads, what was the address of their office?

A Their office was at 710 Ashbury in San Francisco, not far from the street's intersection with Haight Street. The Haight-Ashbury neighborhood, known to legend simply as "the Haight," started off as a concentration of student housing for the kids at San Francisco State. Add a head shop, the Avalon Ballroom, and other groovy attractions, and the Haight quickly became the epicenter of hippie culture; as the psychedelic goings on there were publicized nationwide, it became a magnet for American young people who wanted to get in on the trip.

Q While we're at it, give the etymology of the word "psychedelic."

A The two roots are from the Greek: "psyche," for the mind or soul, and "delos," clear or visible. So psychedelic literally translates as "making the mind or soul clear and visible." The *American Heritage Dictionary* gives this decidedly less-trippy definition: "Of, characterized by, or generating hallucinations, distortions of perception, altered states of awareness, and occasionally states resembling psychosis."

Q Who popularized the term "psychedelic"?

A Enshrined in the title of the 1964 book by acid gurus Timothy Leary, Richard Alpert, and Ralph Metzner, *The Psychedelic Experience,* the word was soon applied to music, fashion, and anything painted in day-glo colors.

Q The Dead's lease at Olompali ran out after June 1966. If the ghosts of Miwok Indians may have been lingering about their adobe home, whose spirit pervaded the next place they moved to?

A The Girl Scouts of America. The ranch they moved to near Lagunitas used to be a Girl Scout camp. It was rural enough, with a pretty little stream running through the property; but it was just down the road from the county sheriff's house, which put a crimp in the partying. When the septic system broke down a few months later, the band was forced to move again.

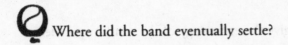

Q Where did the band eventually settle?

A They moved in to the house on 710 Ashbury that Scully had obtained as an office, and the place became Grateful Dead central, hosting an assortment of band members, crew, friends, and hangers-on over the next few years.

Q The Grateful Dead released a single in August 1966. What was on the two sides?

A The disc, produced by the minuscule Scorpio Records, featured two of the band's electrified jug numbers, "Don't Ease Me In" and "Stealin.'"

Q Was the record a hit?

A Given that only about 150 copies of the single were pressed and the only places one could purchase it were a couple of Haight Street head shops, it didn't make much of a dent in the charts.

Q Their record sales weren't the only bummer that summer. What else happened?

A Their first performances outside the United States occurred in late July at the British Colombia Festival in Vancouver, and were marked by a crew member with an arrest record being turned back at the Canadian border and the band almost missing a show while tripping on the Pacific shore. The band also got fed up with the fussy unreliability of Bear's equipment, which led to the end of his position as the Grateful Dead's sound manager, though he would continue his technological involvement with the band.

Q Where did Bear's equipment end up?

A It became the permanent sound system at the Fillmore. Without the wear and tear of travel, it performed much better.

Q That same August, the band was approached by another record company. Which one?

A A friend convinced Joe Smith, president of Warner Brothers Records, to attend a Grateful Dead show at the Avalon Ballroom. Warner Brothers' biggest acts at the time had been Frank Sinatra, Connie Francis, and the Everly Brothers, but Smith was impressed by the Dead, and offered them the chance to record. Garcia and company were suspicious of the record company mogul, but they wanted to make an album, so they agreed. They would record for Warner Brothers for the first few years of their career, becoming the label's first rock band and helping transform Warner into a rock music powerhouse.

Q In September, a poster for a Grateful Dead show at the Avalon featured a striking image. What was it?

A Artists Alton Kelly and Stanley "Mouse" Miller were searching for inspiration in an old edition of *The Rubaiyat of Omar Khayyam,* when they found an illustration of a skeleton wearing a crown of roses. They adapted the image for their poster, the first time roses and bones would come together as a Grateful Dead icon—but by no means the last.

Q Identify the song:
She brings me coffee
She brings me tea
She brings 'bout every damn thing
But the jailhouse key...

A "Don't Ease Me In," another traditional song that began as a staple for Mother McCree's Uptown Jug Champions and lasted throughout the Grateful Dead's career: they recorded a live version in 1966, and released a studio version on the *Go to Heaven* album in 1980.

Q The San Francisco scene changed dramatically after October 6, 1966. What happened on that day?

A LSD became illegal in the State of California. Other states followed suit, and the federal government banned the substance in 1971. The era of open acid tripping was at an end.

Q 1966 ended with another bit of Grateful Dead history. What was it?

A The very first New Year's Eve bash at the Fillmore. The lineup included the cream of the San Francisco music scene, including the Jefferson Airplane, Quicksilver Messenger Service, and, of course, the Grateful Dead. The Dead would play Bill Graham's annual New Years Eve gig for many years to come.

Q After they finished their gig at the Avalon that night, Country Joe and the Fish stopped by the Fillmore and jammed with members of the Grateful Dead and Quicksilver Messenger Service. What was the name they made up for this one-set-only band?

A The Dead Silverfish.

Q On January 14, 1967, the Grateful Dead played at an event that would be recognized as a defining moment in the cultural history of the era. What was the occasion?

A The Human Be-In at the Polo Field in Golden Gate Park. Advertised as "a gathering of the tribes," the event brought together all elements of the San Francisco scene. It featured poets like Gary Snyder and Allen Ginsberg, acid gurus like Timothy Leary and Richard Alpert, peaceniks like Jerry Rubin and toughs like the Hells Angels, and Bear handing out a special batch of acid cooked up for the occasion. But what the 20,000 people in attendance dug most was the music; as the now-famous posters advertising the Be-In had promised, "All San Francisco Bands" were there, including our heroes.

Q How many cops were required to control a crowd of that size?

A Despite the many people and the copious supply of drugs, there was no violence, and two cops on horseback were the entire security contingent. The Love Generation had arrived.

Q At the end of January, the Dead went to the RCA recording studios in Los Angeles to record. How long did it take them to record the bulk of the album?

A Four days; on the fifth, they mixed. It was a generally unpleasant experience for the band; they were intimidated by the surroundings and didn't respond well to the controlled, low-volume recording techniques the engineers imposed on them. The rush was probably brought on by their desire to get out of there—that and the Ritalin that most of the band members were high on during the sessions.

Q Afterward, the band regretted how deferential they had been to their producer, Dave Hassinger. What previous San Francisco band had Hassinger produced? And what iconic rock single was he responsible for?

A The Dead had requested to work with Hassinger, who produced the Jefferson Airplane's album, *Surrealistic Pillow.* Hassinger's praises will forever be sung in Rock 'n' Roll Heaven for producing the Rolling Stones' hit, "Satisfaction."

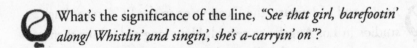

Q What's the significance of the line, *"See that girl, barefootin'
along/ Whistlin' and singin', she's a-carryin' on"*?

A They are the first words of the first song on the first Grateful
Dead album. The band wrote "The Golden Road (to Unlimited
Devotion)" when the Warner Brothers executives complained
that they didn't hear a potential hit single in the material they
had recorded. "The Golden Road" didn't last long in the Dead's
repertoire, but its lyrics captured the Haight-Ashbury scene and
nowadays appear to herald the Summer of Love:
Take a vacation, fall out for a while,
Summer's comin' in, and it's goin' outta style
Well lie down smokin', honey,
Have yourself a ball...

Q Ph.Deadhead Level Question: Where did the name "The
Golden Road (to Unlimited Devotion)" originate?

A If you guessed that it was the title of a work of Eastern mysti-
cism, good try. It was actually a name that had been proposed
by their friend, Sue Swanson, for the Grateful Dead fan club
she was helping to organize.

Q Which perennial Dead favorite contains a reference to "Joe Brown's coal mine"?

A "Beat It On Down the Line," penned by Bay Area blues veteran Jesse Fuller and recorded for the band's first album, *Grateful Dead* (1967). One of the Dead's many musical experiments was to vary the number of beats in the drum introduction. There really was a Joe Brown, who, along with being the president of the Dade Coal Company, was four times elected governor of Georgia in the late 19th century.

Q What's the next line?
Well, can't you see that you're killing each other's soul
You're both out in the streets and you got no place to go
Your constant battles are getting to be a bore . . .

A *So go somewhere else and continue your cream puff war.*
Jerry Garcia's "Cream Puff War" was included on the band's eponymous first album in 1967, and then dropped from the Dead's live repertoire almost as soon as the album was released. Jerry was obviously influenced by Dylan's caustic put-down songs, such as "Like a Rolling Stone" and "Positively 4th Street."

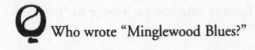

Q Who wrote "Minglewood Blues?"

A Noah Lewis, harmonica player for Cannon's Jug Stompers, the group that first recorded the song in 1928. Lewis later re-recorded the song as a solo act, and called it the "New Minglewood" Blues. Garcia, Weir, and Pigpen learned the song during their jug band days, and the version the Dead premiered in 1967 was dubbed the "New, New Minglewood Blues." Minglewood was a tough company town near Memphis known for its lawless partying.

Q By early 1967, Jerry and Sara's marriage was pretty much over. Who was the young single mother to whom the Dead's lead guitarist now turned his attention? And who was the father of her child?

A Carolyn Adams, who, during her time with the Merry Pranksters, had acquired the Pranksters name Mountain Girl. Her outdoorsy good looks and determined personality had impressed all the band members, as they first encountered her managing light and sound equipment amid the hallucinogenic chaos of the Acid Tests. She left the Pranksters in late 1966 and showed up at 710 Ashbury, with her daughter by Ken Kesey, Sunshine, and a kilo of Acapulco Gold marijuana in tow. By early 1967, Mountain Girl and Jerry were lovers, and moved in together.

Q *The Grateful Dead* was released on St. Patrick's Day, 1967. What kind of critical reaction did it receive?

A The consensus was that the band didn't sound as good on the record as they did live. It was an opinion that became a critical cliché about the Dead over the years, as the spontaneous collective creativity of the band's concerts proved difficult to re-create in the confines of a recording studio.

Q "If you're going to San Francisco," Scott McKenzie sang from every transistor radio in the spring of 1967, "summertime will be a love-in there." Was it?

A Like much of what we think we remember about American culture in the 1960s, The Summer of Love mythology leavens a little fact with a whole lot of hype and wishful thinking. It is true that young people from all over the country flocked to San Francisco to be part of the cultural revolution underway there. When they got to Haight-Ashbury, however, what they found didn't quite match the scene depicted in the festival posters. The crush of kids with no money and no place to stay overwhelmed the little community; the police, who had been tolerant previously, began to crack down on unlawful assemblies in the streets and parks. Unscrupulous people saw drifting youngsters with a taste for drugs as the perfect targets for exploitation. And methedrine, along with other kinds of "speed," began to take the place of LSD as the high of choice, leaving a pack of strung-out addicts in its wake. While the rest of the nation saw San Francisco through day-glo-colored glasses in 1967, the residents of the Haight were watching the idyllic space they had created deteriorate into a serious downer.

Q What slogan began showing up on posters around the Haight with the rise of methedrine use?

A "Speed Kills."

Q What was special about the gig the band played on June 1, 1967?

A While the rest of the Love Generation was heading to California, the Grateful Dead went east. On June 1, they played a free concert in Tompkins Square Park in lower Manhattan, their first-ever gig in New York.

Q At which famous music venue did the Dead play most of its New York gigs in 1967?

A The Café au Go Go, the premier rock club in the Big Apple, home to groups like the Velvet Underground and the Mothers of Invention. It was the exact opposite of the ballroom environment the band was used to: small, dingy, and featuring both horrendous acoustics and a high cover charge; the club didn't even allow dancing.

Q During their New York sojourn, a prep-school buddy of Bob Weir's got the band invited to the mansion home of Billy and Peggy Hitchcock, heirs to the Andrew Mellon family fortune. Who else was a houseguest?

A Timothy Leary, who had turned the Hitchcock mansion, Millbrook, into a psychedelic salon where his acolytes were treated to the acid guru's chemically influenced dogma, based loosely on the Tibetan *Book of the Dead*.

Q The band members found Leary's cosmic priesthood trip a bit of a drag, but they were very intrigued by something else they encountered during their stay at Millbrook. What was it?

A It was the first time they heard the Beatles' album *Sgt. Pepper's Lonely Hearts Club Band*.

The Grateful Dead in 1969, augmented by Mickey Hart (right)
and Tom Constanten (left).

CHAPTER FOUR

Doin' the New Speedway Boogie

By 1967, you didn't have to go to San Francisco to see hippies anymore. They were everywhere, on the move, searching for the scene. The love-in had spilled beyond the confines of ballrooms and began to fill fairgrounds and farmers' fields; the age of the rock festival had begun. What was once the local neighborhood culture of Haight-Ashbury was quickly becoming a national youth movement, as kids from middle class families in the American heartland put on military jackets and go-go boots, painted rainbows on their faces, and turned their backs on what had previously passed for Western Civilization. And for many, Grateful Dead music was the soundtrack to an era in which it seemed like love and music really might save the world.

But along with the ecstasy inevitably came the bad trips, as the cosmic adventurers discovered the dark cloud behind the rainbow. Garcia and company couldn't remain the neighborhood band ready to play the impromptu free show in the park; whether they wanted it or not, the weird, heavy mantle of rock stardom was draped on their shoulders. They had record contracts, concert schedules, and a growing musical family to feed. The Grateful Dead was now a business, in the process of becoming an institution.

Q Name the June 1967 festival that featured such diverse acts as The Association, Ravi Shankar, The Byrds, Hugh Masekela, Otis Redding, and Booker T. and the MGs.

A If you didn't immediately identify the Monterey Pop Festival, you need to do a bit more studying. Organized by John Phillips of the Mamas and the Papas and promoted by Beatles publicist Derek Taylor, the festival brought together the premier pop music acts of the time and was the subject of one of the most famous rockumentaries in all of human history, *Monterey Pop*.

Q Guild Guitars had a promotional tent at the festival. While hanging out there, Bob Weir got into a little jam session with a short white guy on acoustic guitar and a freaky-looking black guy on electric guitar. Who was Bob jamming with?

A The short guy was folk rock star Paul Simon, who'd already had a number of hits with his partner, Art Garfunkel. The black guy, with whom Bob got into a feedback-squealing contest, would soon be known to the world as Jimi Hendrix.

Q Name the bands that preceded and followed the Grateful Dead at the Monterey Pop Festival.

A It was a tough lineup for the Dead. They went on in the aftermath of the Who, who left the stage amid the rubble of Pete Townsend's smashed guitar and Keith Moon's trashed drum kit. Phil Lesh responded to the Who's set with dismay: "We have to follow this?" After a lackluster performance by the Dead (which was interrupted by hundreds of gate crashers who thought the Beatles had arrived), the crowd was introduced to the incendiary Jimi Hendrix Experience. Many in the audience had their first taste of Jimi's virtuoso psychedelic blues guitar; and if that weren't enough to blow them away, Hendrix finished by setting his Fender Stratocaster on fire.

Q Both the Who and Hendrix are featured in D.A. Pennebaker's famous documentary film about the Monterey festival. Where are the Dead?

A The film was originally shot as a television special for ABC. The band distrusted the festival promoters and the film producers, and were horrified by the prospect that footage over which they would have no control would be shown on national TV. As a result, they refused to give their permission to be filmed. Pennebaker ran his cameras for a short part of the Dead's performance anyway, but the band never relented in their refusal to let the footage be used.

Q A major milestone in the development of the Grateful Dead occurred at a dance lesson. Explain.

A At the end of September 1967, the band played a series of shows at a new San Francisco venue called The Straight. The establishment had thrown a few concerts, but Haight audiences wanted to dance, and The Straight couldn't get the necessary license from the city to run a dance club. One of the club's organizers realized that no license was necessary to open a dance instruction studio, so the Dead played for the club's first "dance lesson" on September 29. The next night, Bill Kreutzmann brought along a new friend he'd met at a concert a month earlier, and asked him to sit in with the band. It was the first appearance of Mickey Hart with the Grateful Dead.

Q Who was on the bill at the concert at which Bill met Mickey?

A Count Basie and his Orchestra.

Q What was Mickey Hart's birth name?

A Michael Steven Hartman was born on September 11, 1943, in Flatbush, Brooklyn, the only permanent band member to have grown up outside of California. His father later changed the family surname because he thought it sounded too German, hardly an asset during World War II.

Q How did Mickey come by his love of rhythm?

A Genetics probably had a good deal to do with it. Both his father, Lenny, and his mother, Leah, were marching band drummers, who teamed up to win the doubles drumming competition at the 1939 World's Fair.

Q Did Lenny and Leah provide a stable home for their son?

A Scarcely. Lenny left home before Mickey was born, and was an infrequent figure in the boy's childhood. His mother remarried several times, and Mickey had the usual conflicts with his step-fathers. Mickey himself was a hyperactive kid whose chief talent as a young child was getting into trouble at school.

Q One of the defining moments of Mickey Hart's life occurred when he was ten years old. What was it?

A He saw his father in a movie newsreel about the 1939 World's Fair; it was his first awareness of Lenny's accomplishments as a drummer. Mickey went home and found his dad's drumsticks and practice pad, and a lifelong love affair was born. As he later wrote, "From the age of ten on, all I did was drum. Obsessively. Passionately. Painfully."

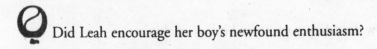

Q Did Leah encourage her boy's newfound enthusiasm?

A Not at first. She tried hiding the sticks and pad from Mickey, but he'd always find them, and sneak into a closet to practice. When she realized there was no dissuading her son, she gave him his first drum lessons.

Q What was young Mickey's first foray outside of marching band music?

A He discovered the classic big band album *Carnegie Hall Jazz Concert,* and was entranced by Gene Krupa's iconic drum solo on "Sing, Sing, Sing." With his characteristic obsessive intensity, Mickey sat down and taught himself to play the complicated piece, one lick at a time. It was the kind of dedication that would win him first chair in the New York All-State Band while he was still a young teenager.

Q What did Mickey do after high school?

A He joined the air force in 1960 before finishing his senior year, hoping to get involved in its crack military bands. He was stationed in Spain, where he augmented his military percussion with involvement in small combos. Mickey also became proficient enough in judo to compete at a high level, and martial arts training only deepened his intense focus.

What brought Mickey Hart to California?

He had tracked down his father, who was running a music store in a suburb of San Francisco; and on Mickey's release from the air force, Lenny invited him to come work at the store. The move to the Bay Area brought Mickey into contact with the burgeoning pop music scene, and it wasn't long before he encountered both LSD and Bill Kreutzmann. After his first sit-in with the Dead at the Straight, Mickey quit the music store and moved in with Bill.

What was the first Grateful Dead song with lyrics by Robert Hunter?

"Alligator," which appears on the *Anthem of the Sun* album and was a regular part of Grateful Dead performances between 1967 and 1971. Although Hunter would soon provide lyrics for Jerry Garcia's songs, the melody of "Alligator" is credited to Phil Lesh and Pigpen, who also contributed lyrics.

Where had Hunter been all this time?

 Living in Palo Alto with his literary ambitions and nursing an addiction to methedrine. When the drug gave him hepatitis, he escaped to New Mexico, where he tried to drink away the symptoms of speed withdrawal. He was a wreck when Garcia contacted him in Taos and asked for his help writing lyrics for "Alligator," and it took him weeks to hitchhike to San Francisco. When Hunter arrived, Jerry played the opening strains of the song, and the lyrics began flowing from Hunter's pen. Garcia liked them, and Robert Hunter had discovered his life's work.

 Which frequent Dead venues are threatened with violence in "Alligator?"

 Bill Graham's Fillmore and the Family Dog's Avalon. Hunter claimed that the lines *Tear down the Fillmore/Gas the Avalon* were contributed by the band, and the song contains no specific explanation for the proposed attacks. Perhaps the song's theme—trying to avoid the continual "bother" of the ever-returning alligator—might be a veiled reference to the hassle of dealing with concert promoters.

Q Identify the song:
I went down to see a gypsy woman just one day, yes I did
I wanna find out
What's wrong with me and my baby
We ain't been getting down like we used to do...

A The words are from Pigpen's studio recording of "Caution
(Do Not Stop on Tracks)" that appears on the *Anthem of the
Sun* album. Like the bluesman he was, Pigpen improvised many
variations of the lyrics over the years.

Q What was Garcia's interpretation of the following lyrics, from
Pigpen's show-closing rave-up, "Turn On Your Love Light?"
She's got box-back nitties
And great big noble thighs
Working undercover with a boar hog's eye...

A If you answered "I don't know," you're right! Journalist Blair
Jackson quoted Garcia as saying: "Don't ask me—I don't know
what the fuck that's all about. It's some weird mojo shit or
something. But he could always pull that shit out."

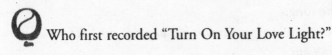

Q Who first recorded "Turn On Your Love Light?"

A It was a hit for blues great Bobby "Blue" Bland in 1962. It's featured on a number of Dead live albums, and was later recorded by Jerry Lee Lewis, Bob Seeger, and Greg Allman. Pigpen's bluesy, raunchy improvisation closed many shows up until his death in 1973. The Dead revived the number in 1981, with Bob Weir on vocals.

Q What quintessential Dead icon appears for the first time in the lyrics of "The Other One?"

A The rose: *Spanish lady come to me, she lays on me this rose/ It rainbow spirals round and round/It trembles and explodes.*

Q What are the two sections of "The Other One?"

A "Cryptical Envelopment," the Jerry Garcia song that contains the refrain *He had to die,* and "The Faster We Go, The Rounder We Get," words by Weir and music by Weir and Bill Kreutzmann, with the refrain *Comin', comin', comin' around, comin' around in a circle.* "Cryptical Envelopment" is reprised as an ending. "The Other One" was one of the first long-form psychedelic jam pieces that established the Grateful Dead's characteristic style of group improvisation.

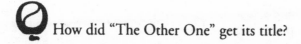

Q How did "The Other One" get its title?

A The band developed its first long-form improvisation in 1967 around two pieces. "Dark Star" had a title; the other piece didn't, or rather, it had a profusion of possible titles, including "Quodlibet for Tenderfeet." So the second piece was typically referred to as "the other one," a name that stuck.

Q Of the countless joints smoked by the band family over the decades, which might be the most influential?

A The one handed to Robert Hunter in Golden Gate Park in September 1967. Noticing Hunter scribbling lyrics on a park bench, a hippie walked up and offered him a toke, saying, "Here, maybe this will make things easier for you." Hunter took a hit, and then finished the lyrics to the Greatful Dead's most important anthem, "Dark Star." The open-ended modal progression was perfect for endless modification, and accommodated every mood from quiet introspection to thunderous crescendos of electric noise. Nearly two hundred recorded performances of the song survive on tape.

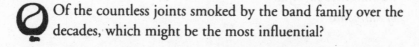

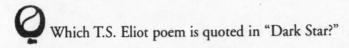

Q Which T.S. Eliot poem is quoted in "Dark Star?"

A "Let us go then, you and I/When the evening is spread out against the sky/Like a patient etherized upon a table" is the opening of Eliot's most famous poem, *The Love Song of J. Alfred Prufrock*. Robert Hunter displays his literary chops with this echo:
Shall we go,
you and I
while we can?
Through
the transitive nightfall
of diamonds...

Q The afternoon of October 2, 1967 saw another first for the Grateful Dead. What was the historic event?

A Their first drug bust. An informant slipped into 710 Ashbury and asked to smoke a joint. No sooner did the weed come out than the law came in and took Bob, Pigpen, Scully and Rifkin, and a pack of others in attendance, off to detention as TV cameras captured the scene for the evening news. The cops got a pound of marijuana, a little hashish, and Pigpen's pistol.

Q Danny Rifkin was never much of a writer, so he got a friend to write the news release the band handed out at a press conference the day after the bust. Who wrote the release, and what was his later contribution to rock 'n' roll?

A It was Danny's college pal, Harry Shearer, who went on to become a comic writer for TV, a regular voice actor on *The Simpsons,* and, of course, to portray bass player Derek Smalls in the "mockumentary" film, *This is Spinal Tap.*

Q As a result of the bust, Rock Scully was fined $200. Pigpen and Bob Weir were only fined $100 each. Why the reduced penalty?

A They hadn't actually been smoking pot at the time of the raid.

Q In December, the band headed to New York to do more recording for the *Anthem of the Sun* album, and hired a new roadie to handle the equipment on the trip. Did he hang around long?

A Indeed he did. Their new crew member was Larry "Ram Rod" Shurtliff, a former Merry Prankster who'd earned his road credentials riding shotgun for Neal Cassady aboard Further. He would go on to be chief of their road crew, shepherding the band's ever larger and complex mass of gear and sound-system equipment through the long strange trip to come.

Q On February 18, 1968, there was a riot in Haight-Ashbury that pitted cops with tear gas and riot sticks against hippies throwing bottles. Trying to calm tempers, the city planned some music events for March 3, and ordered Haight Street closed to traffic. How did the Grateful Dead respond?

A With a particularly in-your-face bit of civil disobedience. They managed to get a couple of flatbed trucks past the barricades, and used them as a stage to perform an impromptu free concert right in the middle of the "closed" street, as the Hells Angels provided a defensive perimeter. Music resounded through the neighborhood, and thousands filled Haight Street. As Phil Lesh recalled, "It wasn't anything like an audience, man, it was like an outdoors acid test with more people."

Q Who produced the Grateful Dead's second album?

A David Hassinger tried; but unlike their first recording experience, the band was not about to be pushed around. They insisted on recording the material they wanted in the way they wanted to do it. Their demands for unusual effects and refusal to follow the standard pop music recording format drove Hassinger nuts, and he quit. Garcia and Lesh finished the job themselves.

Q What complicated bit of audio wizardry did Jerry and Phil produce for the *Anthem of the Sun* album?

A One of their experiments was to overlay several live recordings of "The Other One," creating a billowing explosion of sound.

Q Speaking of "The Other One," the suite is conceived in two parts, as we've discussed. On the album notes for *Anthem of the Sun*, however, the piece has four different titles. Why?

A So that the band would be able to collect recording royalties for more than just one song.

Q None of the long, strange cuts on *Anthem of the Sun* were really hit single material, but Warner Brothers released a single anyway. What was on it?

A A cut-down, two-minute version of "Dark Star," backed with Bob Weir's song, "Born Cross-Eyed." Being released by a major record label didn't have a lot of effect on the success of their second single; it sold a total of 500 copies.

Q What was the business venture the Dead launched in 1968 with the Jefferson Airplane and Quicksilver Messenger Service?

A The groups formed a company to lease and operate the Carousel Ballroom on the corner of Market and Van Ness in San Francisco. The idea was that all three bands would play the Carousel for free and split the profits. The partnership was largely a scam to get the lease; in practice, it was the Dead's operation, and it became a home-away-from-home for the band and its growing family of crew and friends. The Carousel became the epicenter of the San Francisco Sound, but the group's laid-back business attitude pretty much guaranteed its failure.

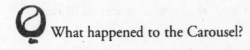

Q What happened to the Carousel?

A Bill Graham bought it when the original Fillmore auditorium closed, and reopened the Carousel as the Fillmore West.

Q The band had a tense meeting in August 1968. What was on the agenda?

A The firing of Bob Weir and Pigpen. In light of the band's increasingly complex improvisations, Garcia, Lesh, and Hart were dissatisfied with what they felt was Bob's lackadaisical attitude and guitar playing; Pigpen's blues just didn't fit in with the new music, and his continual drunkenness was causing problems. Although they didn't utter the words "you're fired" (we know, because Bear taped the meeting), they made it abundantly clear that they didn't want Bob and Pigpen around anymore.

Q Did the firing take?

A Of course not. Despite the hostile exchange, there was never any serious attempt to expel the two, and Bob and Pigpen continued to perform with the band.

Q Identify the song:
I go on, I go on, I can't fill my cup
There's a hole in the bottom, the well has dried up...

A "Clementine," a Hunter/Lesh collaboration that is considerably darker than the folk song everyone learns in school. The Dead used their version as a transition piece in jam sequences in 1968 and '69, but never recorded a studio version.

Q What are the four cats mentioned in "China Cat Sunflower?"

A The first is the one in the title, of course, reminiscent of the porcelain Satsuma decorative figures made in Japan since the 17th century. Next, Krazy Kat arrives in the second verse, the character in George Herman's surreal comic strip from the early 20th century. Then comes the Cheshire Cat, presumably the one from Lewis Carroll's *Alice in Wonderland,* although the one in the song lacks a smile (and one eye). The last line mentions Queen Chinee, one of the title pets in Edith Sitwell's poem *Trio for Two Cats and a Trombone.*

Q What's the hidden meaning of the title of the song "The Eleven?"

A You will search the song's lyrics for it in vain. The title refers to the time signature of the song, which is composed in the very strange 1 1/4 time. The number was the product of the band's musical experiments, initiated by Mickey Hart's meeting with Indian percussionist Alla Rakha, which involved trying out time signatures that were never used in pop music before or since.

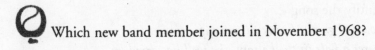

Q Which new band member joined in November 1968?

A It was Tom Constanten, T.C. for short, Phil Lesh's pal who had just gotten out of the air force. Constanten took over on keyboards, where his more versatile, cerebral approach seemed to fit the band's new music better than Pigpen's blues organ.

Q Where did that leave Pigpen?

A Off to one side of the stage, pounding on conga drums. Pig didn't fade into obscurity, though; after a night of psychedelic explorations of strange new musical worlds, the Dead would often bring Pigpen on to close the show with a blues raver like "Turn On Your Love Light." Pigpen's soul instincts continued to ground the band's music and keep it from floating off into musical abstraction.

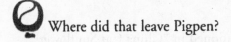

Q What song are these lyrics from?
Tell B for the beast at the ending of the wood
Well it eat all the children that would not be good...

A The lines are from the Bahamian gospel song, "And We Bid You Goodnight," that the band often sang a capella as a coda to its shows in the late '60s and early '70s.

Q For extra points, identify what biblical story the lines refer to.

A You're a real Dead scholar if you recognize the reference to II Kings in the Old Testament, in which bears rush from the woods to slaughter children who had been mocking the prophet Elijah.

Q In late January 1969, the Dead played a series of seven shows at the Avalon and Fillmore West. What was special about them?

A They produced the first live 16-track recordings ever made. Ampex had just introduced the first 16-track recording machines, and the band fell in love with them. The loud volume of rock music and the iffy acoustics of many halls had made recording live rock performances difficult. With the new technology, each voice and instrument could be individually recorded and mixed, permitting a clarity of sound that made the end product nearly as listenable as studio tapes. Sixteen-track taping made it possible for the Grateful Dead to at last capture the magic of their live performances, and the album that resulted from those seven shows was immediately hailed as a masterpiece.

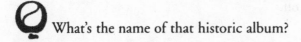

Q What's the name of that historic album?

A *Live/Dead,* released by Warner Brothers in 1969.

Q In April 1969, the band hired a new business manager. Who was he, and what had he been doing previously?

A It was Mickey Hart's dad, Lenny. After running the music store, Lenny had taken on the role of a traveling fundamentalist preacher, which lent a certain evangelistic edge to his business dealings. Mickey was thrilled to have his father back in his life, but Lenny Hart freaked some of the band family out, including Bear, who had seen enough southern preachers to have serious doubts.

Q Besides a new business manager, Mickey also brought the band a new hangout. What and where was it?

A The band began spending a lot of time at the horse ranch Mickey was renting in Novato. Next to drumming, riding horses was the love of Mickey's life; he especially loved going on long rides with his horse, Snorter, and his dog, Glups, during which all three were fortified with lysergic acid.

Q What was Jerry Garcia's favorite morning ritual?

A He could often be found on a couch in front of the TV, running scales on the guitar while watching *Captain Kangaroo* with the sound off.

Q Warner Brothers released the Dead's third album, *Aoxomoxoa*, in June 1969. What was the promotional gimmick their ad people came up with?

A They ran a Pigpen look-alike contest, designed as a send-up of teen fan magazines.

Q What does *Aoxomoxoa* mean, and what language is it in?

A Psych! The word is a meaningless palindrome (it's spelled the same way backwards as forwards, man), created by the album cover artist, Rick Griffin. The band originally wanted to call the album "Earthquake Country."

Q What's the next line?
Wishing well with a golden bell
Bucket hanging clear to Hell
Hell halfway 'twixt now and then . . .

A *Stephen fill it up and lower down and lower down again.*
The Stephen in question of course is "St. Stephen," a song that appeared on the *Aoxomoxoa* album in 1969. Robert Hunter said that the title character wasn't based on any historical individual, which would explain why the details of the song don't seem to have much to do with the Stephen whose martyrdom is recorded in the book of Acts, nor to any of the other half dozen or so St. Stephens on record. Some San Franciscans thought it might have been a reference to Stephen Gaskin, a Haight Street notable who went on to found a commune in Tennessee known as The Farm.

Q Who wrote "Not Fade Away?"

A The song is credited to Buddy Holly and his manager, Norman Petty. Holly released it as the B-side of "Oh, Boy" in 1957. Seven years later, it was the Rolling Stones' first hit in the United States. The Dead often combined the song with "Goin' Down the Road" in the early '70s, whipping it to a frenzy that neither Holly nor the Stones ever attempted.

Q Which was the first Dead song to mention "truckin'"?

A "Cosmic Charlie," which appears on the *Aoxomoxoa* album, begins *Cosmic Charlie, how do you do?/Truckin' in style along the avenue.* Truckin' was a shuffling two-step dance from the 1920s, the name of which made it into several blues standards, including "Blind Boy Fuller's Truckin' My Blues Away."

Q Who first popularized the word "truckin'"?

A By 1969, the underground cartoonist R. Crumb had already revived the term with his *Keep on Truckin'* drawing in Zap Comics. It would resurface a little later in another Grateful Dead number you may have heard.

Q Which song features Tom Banjo and the Marsh King's daughter?

A They join Electra and the Carrion Crow in Robert Hunter's ethereal and eclectic lyrics to "Mountains of the Moon." The words pack in references to Japanese poetry, Greek mythology, English fairy stories, American folk songs, and a Hans Christian Andersen story.

Q The Grateful Dead were on the bill at the greatest rock music festival of all time. We'll start with the gimme question: name the location of the festival.

A If you couldn't come up with Woodstock, New York, August 15-18, 1969, you are either very young or extraterrestrial. More than 400,000 people showed up for what was the largest musical gathering in history and the defining moment of a generation.

Q Next level: Name the unknown San Francisco band that launched its career at Woodstock.

A Santana, which introduced Latin rhythms and one of the greatest electric guitarists to rock music.

Q Ultimate Peace, Love, and Music-level question: What was the opening number the Grateful Dead played at Woodstock?

A "St. Stephen," and they made a botch of it. The band was intimidated by numerous equipment problems (including major electric shocks from their microphones), the blazing stage lights, and the pressure of having to perform before such a teeming multitude; and thus, they never quite got it together during their Woodstock set. Jerry Garcia is reputed to have said afterward, "It's nice to know you can blow the biggest gig of your career and it doesn't matter."

Q Woodstock is sacred to cherished memory as the highest moment of '60s youth culture (in many more ways than one). The nadir followed soon after. What was it?

A The free music concert at the Altamont Speedway near Livermore, California. Held less than four months after the legendary festival on Max Yasgir's farm, the Rolling Stones initiated the Altamont festival as a way of thanking fans for the success of their 1969 American tour (and as an apology for several canceled concert dates). The lineup was stellar— the Stones, of course, Santana, the Jefferson Airplane, Crosby, Stills, Nash and Young, and the Grateful Dead. But any hopes that Altamont would become Woodstock Redux were hideously dashed. In the Merry Pranksters tradition, the Hells Angels were invited to serve as unofficial security; the bikers' violent side went on display, and the day became a rolling series of brutal incidents in which both concertgoers and musicians were beaten. The iconic moment came at the climax of the Stones' set, when a fan with a gun was stabbed to death by an Angel.

Q In what rockumentary can you watch the nightmare of Altamont unfold?

A Featured at the end of the documentary *Gimme Shelter,* about the Stones' '69 tour, Altamont became an emblem of the bad trip on the other side of the Flower Power mystique, and many would see it as the official end of the Love Generation.

Q *Gimme Shelter* was one of a trio of festival documentaries— along with *Monterey Pop* and *Woodstock*—that define the way we think of the late '60s pop music scene. For Dead fans, all three share an unpleasant characteristic. What is it?

A While the Grateful Dead were on the bill at all three festivals, they appear in none of the movies (with the exceptions of a famous Jerry Garcia cameo in *Woodstock*, and a brief glimpse of Garcia and Lesh in *Gimme Shelter*). With the Monterey and Woodstock events, the band's suspicions over quality and artistic control dissuaded them from giving permission for their sets to be used in the documentaries. At Altamont, the decision was more straightforward: After arriving by helicopter at the speedway, they learned about the chaotic situation and decided not to go on.

Q Before we leave the topic, what was Jerry's line in *Woodstock?*

A After taking a hit from a joint, Garcia holds it before the camera and says, "Marijuana. Exhibit A." The quip, in which Jerry appears to label the evidence to be used against him, can also be heard on the *Woodstock* soundtrack album.

Q The Grateful Dead got neither a festival performance nor a film appearance out of the Altamont festival, but they did get a song out of it. What was it?

A "New Speedway Boogie," from the *Workingman's Dead* album. As a matter of principle, the band didn't do topical songs or protest music. But after an article by rock critic Ralph Gleason accused the Dead of being responsible for the disastrous decision to invite the Hells Angels to Altamont, Hunter and Garcia had to respond. In the song, the Dead's boogie bounce takes a few troubled turns to minor chords, and the lyrics express the group's characteristic gentle fatalism about human reality:
Spent a little time on the mountain
Spent a little time on the hill
I saw things getting out of hand
I guess they always will...

But there's also optimism in the face of tragedy:
One way or another
One way or another
One way or another
This darkness got to give...

Q "New Speedway Boogie" is yet another tasty tune on one of the most loved Grateful Dead studio albums. Was the song a concert favorite?

A No. The Dead performed the song live at the Fillmore in San Francisco just a few days after it was written, then played it in concert for less than a year before dropping it entirely for two decades. It was one of a number of oldies that were revived for concerts in the 1990s.

Q The band recorded another ominous song in the wake of Altamont, which would go unreleased until the rarities collection, *So Many Roads*, made its appearance many years later. What was it? If you need another hint, the song has gruesome echoes of the nursery rhyme about Solomon Grundy.

A "Mason's Children," by Hunter and Garcia. Mason is "a mighty man," a classic patriarch whose children can't be trusted. They brick him up in a wall on Monday, they dig him up on Tuesday, and cook up a stew with unspecified ingredients (the old man?) on Thursday. That feast is illuminated by "fires tall and bright," reminiscent of the bonfires lighting the evil scene at Altamont.

Q Besides the two songs, the Grateful Dead got something else out of its participation in superfestivals like Woodstock and Altamont. What was this graphic icon?

A Always obsessing over the band's equipment, Bear became unnerved by the fact that the large collection of acts at a big festival meant a lot of identical-looking gear cases being mixed together. He needed a simple design that could be spray-painted on cases to identify the Dead's equipment. Bear turned to artist Bob Thomas, who created an image of a skull seen from above with a lightening bolt in the center. It became one of the most famous band logos ever.

Brent Mydland, front and center, joined the band in 1979.

CHAPTER FIVE

Uncle John's Band

The dreams of the Love Generation had been ground beneath the wheels of Vietnam. Kennedy had been replaced by Nixon, Martin Luther King by the Black Panthers, Woodstock by Altamont. From college campuses to urban ghettos, violent revolution replaced songs of peace and love.

After trips to so many strange new worlds, the Grateful Dead was ready for a little normalcy, both spiritually and musically. The music they would produce in the 1970s can be heard as an expression of the awareness that, when transcendence is too much to ask for, the best you can do is keep trucking on. In three classic albums, they would put away the far-out experimentation and reach for the grounded truths of the music they'd grown up on. The result was a collection of songs that brought smiles in the midst of hard times and laughter in the face of weirdness. Grateful Dead songs became the perfect antidote to an era of fear and loathing, and their lyricism and humor gave them a permanent home in the American songbook.

Long after the rest of the San Francisco bands had either disappeared or succumbed to the homogenizing demands of the pop music industry, the Grateful Dead kept rolling on, despite losses, scams, and an ever-changing lineup. Even in the midst of the slick, insipid Disco Era, a coterie of hardcore fans kept showing up—and growing in number.

Q Identify the two things Jerry Garcia got in 1969 that were to change the course of the band's music.

A A new roommate, and a new instrument. The roommate who moved in with Jerry and Mountain Girl was Robert Hunter, who began churning out lyrics for songs at a prodigious rate. As a result, songs began to replace free-flowing jams as the cornerstone of the band's music. The second acquisition was a pedal steel guitar, the instrument that lends its lush, crying chords to country music. Jerry had been fascinated with the steel guitar for a long time, and now began studying it in earnest. The country feel began to seep into the songs he was writing with Hunter, and the stage was set for the music that many fans most strongly associate with the Grateful Dead.

Q When Hunter and Garcia collaborated on songs, what came first, the words or the music?

A With a few exceptions, the words came first. Hunter would generate a rhyming poem, and Jerry would create a melody to go with it. The songs would then continue to evolve as the band worked them up, with various individuals contributing licks and lyrics.

Q What's steel about a steel guitar?

A It's not the strings or the body; it's the steel bar the guitarist holds in the left hand to fret the strings. The bar is what allows a steel guitarist to create the sweeping glissandos and subtle variations in pitch that give the instrument its expressive quality.

Q What's Jerry Garcia's most famous steel guitar solo?

A Jerry's steel work graces many Dead songs and the music of other bands as well; but the solo you'd probably recognize instantly is the one he lent to the Crosby, Stills & Nash hit, "Teach Your Children." The version you hear on the record is the second take, and Jerry felt he was just warming up. Thanks to the record label restrictions of the day, Jerry Garcia wasn't credited for his contribution to the CS&N classic.

Q Jerry's fascination with country music led to the development of a side project. What was it?

A Jerry got together with Phil Lesh, Mickey Hart, and Jerry's friend John Dawson to create the New Riders of the Purple Sage, a band that played traditional songs and country classics in bars and various small venues around the Bay Area. Eventually, the ensemble would open a few Grateful Dead shows and even record its own material. The membership of the New Riders would change over the years, and Garcia and the other Dead members gradually became less involved; but the band continues to ride the open plains of American music today.

Q For extra trail-dust points, where did the band get its name?

A From the title of a 1912 novel by Western master Zane Grey, *Riders of the Purple Sage.*

Q What was Warner Brothers Records president Joe Smith's first reaction upon hearing *Workingman's Dead?*

A He burst from his office and ran down the hall, shouting, "We've got a single! We've got a single!" After the challengingly complex musical experiments the Dead had recorded for Warner so far, an album full of approachable pop songs was the last thing Smith expected—and he was thrilled.

Q Which song includes the plaintive request, *Don't murder me/ I beg of you, don't murder me?*

A "Dire Wolf," from the *Workingman's Dead* album (1970). The motif of playing cards with a demon makes another appearance in this song, this time in the form of *Canis dirus,* a huge prehistoric wolf.

Q Was the dire wolf "600 pounds of sin," as he's described in the song?

A A bit of an exaggeration. *Canis dirus* was bigger than today's timber wolf, but they never got much heavier than 175 pounds.

Q Jerry Garcia said that the *Don't murder me* refrain was very real to him at the time the song was recorded. Why?

A A serial killer, who identified himself as "Zodiak," was terrorizing the Bay area. Between December 1968 and October 1969, the Zodiak Killer claimed at least five victims. Paul Krassner quoted Garcia as saying, "Every night I was coming home from the studio, and I'd stop at an intersection and look around, and if a car pulled up, it was like, 'This is it, I'm gonna die now.'" The murderer's identity was never uncovered.

Q According to the song, what time did Casey Jones's old engine leave River Junction?

A *Hits River Junction at seventeen to/at a quarter to ten/you know it's trav'lin' again.* Robert Hunter implies that cocaine is the problem in this reworking of the famous myth of Casey Jones's Last Ride.

Q Was there really ever a Casey Jones?

A There really was a John Luther "Casey" Jones, an engineer on the Illinois Central line who smashed his speeding train into another freight on April 30, 1900. His friend, Wallace Saunders, an African–American who also worked on the railroad, wrote a song about the incident. That number became the basis of a ragtime song that was a huge national hit in 1909, and the ill-fated Casey Jones entered American folklore.

Q Which beloved Grateful Dead song was inspired by the Bulgarian Women's Choir?

A "Uncle John's Band," the melodic sing-along that opens *Workingman's Dead*. In a 1991 interview with Blair Jackson, Garcia recalled, "I was listening to records of the Bulgarian Women's Choir and also this Greek-Macedonian music—these penny whistlers—and on one of those records was a song that featured this little turn of melody that was so lovely that I thought, 'Gee, if I could get this into a song it would be so great.' So I stole it."

Q How does the battle flag created by Colonel Christopher Gadsden in 1776 figure into "Uncle John's Band?"

A It's motto is, "Don't Tread on Me." The flag, featuring a coiled rattlesnake, was designed by Gadsden for the commander in chief of the revolutionary American navy.

Q Where is Anne Beauneu from?

A Saint Angel, according to the first verse of the Hunter-Garcia song "Black Peter" from the *Workingman's Dead* album. There don't seem to be historical references to either the name or the place.

Q And while we're on this slow, soulful song, to what very famous individual is Black Peter connected?

A Santa Claus. In the Netherlands, St. Nicholas is part of a team; he's accompanied by a group of sinister Spanish moors, called Black Peters, who carry switches to beat naughty children. In the song however, Black Peter is a figure whose poverty and pain seem to be a source of entertainment.

Q In which song, written for Pigpen by Robert Hunter, is the singer *chippin' up rocks for the great highway?*

A "Easy Wind," from *Workingman's Dead*. Although Bob Weir claimed it was one of his favorite Dead songs, the band only performed it live for about a year after its release.

Q In "Easy Wind," "ballin' the jack" is a euphemism for operating a jackhammer. Where did the phrase come from originally?

A It was the title of a 1913 Dixieland jazz song that instructed listeners in a dance by the same name:
First you put your two knees close up tight
Then you sway 'em to the left
Then you sway 'em to the right
Step around the floor kind of nice and light
Then you twist around and twist around with all your might
Stretch your lovin' arms straight out in space
Then you do the eagle rock with style and grace
Swing your foot way 'round then bring it back
Now that's what I call Ballin' the Jack.

Q Name the legendary jazz trumpeter who opened for the Grateful Dead for three shows at the Fillmore West in April 1970?

A Miles Davis, whose *Kind of Blue* album in 1960 had made him tremendously popular. In 1970 he was in the process of blowing everybody's minds with a funky breed of weird jazz fusion captured on the *Bitches Brew* album. Jerry was a big Miles fan from way back, and the two hit it off famously.

Q The Grateful Dead's second album of tuneful songs with a rootsy, mellow vibe, *American Beauty*, appeared later in 1970. Heads soon noticed something particularly far-out about the cover. What was it?

A Thanks to the lettering, which appears to be some kind of hallucinatory flow of energy, the title of the album looks like it could also be "American Reality." Try it!

Q Ok, numerologists! Enumerate the appearances of the number twenty in the song "Friend of the Devil."

A There are the twenty hounds trailing the song's hero as he lights out from Reno; and the "twenty bills" borrowed from the devil in the second verse becomes the "twenty-dollar bill" His Satanic Majesty reclaims in verse three. By the way, there doesn't seem to be a specific significance to the number 20 in classic western numerology, but it is the product of 10, the number of rebirth, multiplied by 2, the number of balance and union. So maybe he does make it home by daylight.

Q What's the next line?
Come all you pretty women
With your hair a-hanging down
Open up your windows . . .

A *. . . cause the Candyman's in town.* The Candyman is a popular figure in classic blues songs, in which he's usually charming the ladies. In the Hunter-Garcia song from the *American Beauty* album, however, he seems preoccupied with shooting craps.

Q According to the song, of what three things are *The Attics of My Life* full?

A *Cloudy dreams unreal, tastes no tongue can know, and lights no eye can see.* The song was an infrequent feature at concert performances, possibly because the intricate vocal harmonies were difficult to pull off live.

Q Among the many marvelous attributes of the woman described in "Sugar Magnolia," we're told, *She can dance a Cajun rhythm/ Jump like a Willys in four-wheel drive.* What's a Willys?

A The first jeep, built by the Overland Motor Company (founded by John North Willys) for use by the army during World War II. According to legend, if you threw the transmission into gear in just the right way, you could actually make the vehicle jump into the air.

Q Who wrote "Sugar Magnolia?"

A Bob Weir, with a little lyrical help from Robert Hunter.

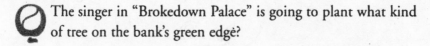

Q The singer in "Brokedown Palace" is going to plant what kind of tree on the bank's green edge?

A A weeping willow. It's a good horticultural choice, because weeping willows do well in wet soil. Hence the tree's Latin species name, *Salix babylonica*, named for the biblical story in which the Hebrews weep by the rivers of Babylon as they are taken in captivity.

Q Pigpen does the lead vocal on what song from *American Beauty*?

A "Operator," for which he also wrote the words and music.

Q The woman Pigpen's trying fruitlessly to telephone in "Operator" might, we are told, be *workin' in a house of blue lights.* What is a house of blue lights?

A No, that's a house of red lights. According to the '40s rhythm and blues song "House of Blue Lights" by Freddie Slack and Don Raye, the joint in question serves up barbecue and hot music.

Q Friedrich Nietzsche, describing the pitfalls of self-determination, wrote, "For he who proceeds on his own path in this fashion encounters no one . . . No one comes along to help him: all the perils, accidents, malice, and bad weather which assail him he has to tackle by himself. For his path is his alone." What *American Beauty* cut might he have been listening to?

A "Ripple," if it had been recorded only 89 years earlier. Nietzsche certainly would have recognized his theme in the lyrics:
There is a road
No simple highway
Between the dawn
And the dark of night
And if you go
No one may follow
That path is for
Your steps alone . . .
. . . if you fall
You fall alone.
If you should stand
Then who's to guide you?

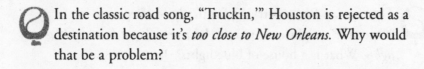

Q In the classic road song, "Truckin,'" Houston is rejected as a destination because it's *too close to New Orleans*. Why would that be a problem?

A The Crescent City was the location of the band's 1970 drug bust. The nasty encounter with the law is described in detail a few lines later:

Sitting and staring out of a hotel window
Got a tip they're gonna kick the door in again
I like to get some sleep before I travel
But if you got a warrant, I guess you're gonna come in
Busted—down on Bourbon Street...

The band vowed never to return to New Orleans after the bust, but they eventually forgave the city and played there several times in the 1980s.

Q How does the toothpaste Pepsodent figure into "Truckin'"?

A Robert Hunter said that a Pepsodent commercial, in which a woman's failure to use the dentifrice leads to a decline in both her smile and health in general, was the inspiration for "Sweet Jane," who has "lost her sparkle" on a diet of reds, vitamin C, and cocaine.

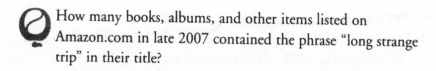

How many books, albums, and other items listed on Amazon.com in late 2007 contained the phrase "long strange trip" in their title?

Fifteen, ranging from the 1977 Grateful Dead compilation album of that name to an article from *Academic Exchange Quarterly* entitled "What a long, strange trip it's been: identity, integrity and the scholarship of teaching."

If two classic rock albums weren't enough for one year, 1970 also saw two notable side projects for Mr. Garcia. What were they?

Jerry wrote and performed the soundtrack music for the film *Zabriskie Point*, by master Italian director Michelangelo Antonioni. The more important landmark for Dead fans, however, was his recording that year of his first solo album, which would be released in 1971. It took a while; other than drums, which were contributed by Bill Kreutzmann, Garcia played all the instruments himself. *Garcia* contains a number of songs that became Grateful Dead performance classics, like "Deal" and "Sugaree."

Q The band's move to a more pop-oriented sound was one of the factors that lead to the departure of keyboardist Tom Constanten in 1970. What was another? (Hint: Think Tom Cruise and John Travolta.)

A T.C. had become a devotee of the Church of Scientology, which forbids drug use—a tough commandment to keep around the Grateful Dead. It's probably no accident that his leaving was decided about the same time as the New Orleans bust went down. Beyond that, however, Constanten had his own artistic vision, and he viewed the Dead as largely Jerry Garcia's backup band.

Q Mickey Hart also quit the band in 1971, and didn't return until 1974. What brought on the hiatus?

A His dad, Lenny, screwed him over one more time. His business dealings as the band's manager grew increasingly fishy. Finally, Ram Rod had had enough, and threatened to quit if Lenny wasn't fired. When Lenny responded to his termination by stealing the band's financial records and fleeing to Mexico, Mickey realized that his father had been cheating them. It turned out that Lenny had stolen more than $150,000 from the Grateful Dead, leaving them essentially broke. Although the other band members didn't hold Mickey responsible for his dad's treachery—they never even pressed charges against Lenny—he blamed himself for bringing a crook into the fold, and left the band. But life with the Dead had too much of a hold on him, and three years later he returned.

Q What did Mickey do to keep himself busy during his absence from the Dead?

A He fronted the Diga Rhythm Band, a huge crew of percussionists that explored rhythm traditions from around the world. Their 1976 album, *Diga*, is one of the earliest examples of the international musical synthesis known as world music.

Q The official name of the band's 1971 live album is *Grateful Dead*. Because of the flower-wreathed skeleton on the album cover, many fans refer to the album as "Skull and Roses." What did the band want to call it?

A "Skullfuck." It was Weir's suggestion, and everybody thought it would be a hoot; when the Warner Brothers executives expressed their horror, the band dug in its heels and insisted. Only when they were convinced that record distributors and chain stores would refuse to carry an album with that name did the Dead relent.

Q Name the husband and wife team who brought a new dimension to the band's music in the 1970s.

A Keith and Donna Godchaux. Keith, whose keyboard work was strongly influenced by jazz and classical music, introduced himself to Jerry Garcia at a gig in 1971 after Donna talked him into it. It just so happened that the band needed a replacement keyboardist for Pigpen, whose health was failing, and they gave Keith an audition. His talent for improvisation and his ability to channel everyone from Bach to Jerry Lee Lewis won him a home with the Dead. A few months later, Donna, herself a talented vocalist, began to perform with the band as well. As the only woman who ever sang regularly with the band, Donna added strength and richness to the Dead's vocal harmonies and a beatific stage presence. But despite their important contributions, all was not harmonious with the Godchauxes. Keith's heavy drug use and the couple's violent marital squabbles eventually caused too much trouble, and they left the band in 1979. A year later, Keith Godchaux died in an automobile accident.

Q During the Grateful Dead's 1972 tour of Europe, the band became very interested in hypnocracy. Explain this philosophical term.

A Gotcha again, man. Hypnocracy was a bit of involved goofing that developed during the long bus trips between shows. The point was to attribute profound-sounding assertions to hypnocracy without ever actually defining it: "In the sea of hypnocracy, the shore is just another wave." As crewmember Willy Legate asked, "Is hypnocracy not the aspiration to know what it is?"

Q What dreadful thing did Ron McKernan have in common with Jack Kerouac?

A They both died of the same cause, internal hemorrhaging of the esophageal vein caused by years of heavy drinking. Pigpen finally had been forced to give up booze when he came down with liver disease, and while he still performed occasionally with the Dead, he was often too sick to tour, and concentrated on writing and recording a solo album. On March 8, 1973, a friend found him dead on the floor of his apartment.

Q How did the band respond to Pigpen's death?

A In a way their old friend would have appreciated: with an over-the-top wake. More than 500 people gathered in and around Bob Weir's home in Mill Valley; the drunken spree was notable for an impromptu orgy that broke out on the hillside and for the band's road manager, Sam Cutler, catching a cream pie in the face.

Q Name the studio album released by the Grateful Dead in 1974.

A No, it's not "Live from the Mars Hotel," or even "From the Mars Hotel." The official name of the album that contains "U.S. Blues," "Scarlet Begonias," "Ship of Fools," and other Dead favorites is *Grateful Dead from the Mars Hotel.*

Q In "U.S. Blues," what's Uncle Sam's pulse?

A *Stays 72, come shine or rain* (a bit elevated, perhaps from all that flag waving and bag popping).

Q Translate the title of the 15th century German satire, *Das Narrenshiff.*

A The "Ship of Fools." As in the Hunter-Garcia song, the image has been used by writers and painters for centuries to symbolize a society adrift and under the control of idiots. It was also the tile of a 1962 novel by Catherine Anne Porter that was made into a movie with an all-star cast three years later.

Q Where does the singer meet the girl with "scarlet begonias" in her hair? And for extra rings and bells, what city would that put him in?

A *As I was walkin' 'round Grosvenor Square . . . .* Grosvenor Square is in London, and is the site of the American embassy.

Q Jerry Garcia toured with a band beside the Grateful Dead in 1973. What was the band's name, and what kind of music did they play?

A Jerry teamed up with his friends David Grisman and Peter Rowan to form Old & in the Way, a project that allowed him to play bluegrass banjo again. On an East Coast tour that year, they traveled with legendary country fiddle player Vassar Clements. Bear's tape of one of their shows became the *Old & in the Way* album, released in 1975.

Q Jerry Garcia's lyricist was usually Robert Hunter. Bob Weir's lyricist was often John Barlow. Who wrote lyrics for the songs composed by Phil Lesh?

A Phil's songwriting partner on numbers like "Pride of Cucamonga" and "Unbroken Chain" was Beat poet and jazz saxophonist Bobby Petersen, an old friend of Phil's and a traveling companion of Neal Cassady.

Q By 1973, the band had broken loose from the constraints of their relationship with Warner Brothers Records; determined to exercise more control over their own destiny, they decided to form their own record label. What was it called? And what was the first Grateful Dead album released on the new label?

A The Dead's attempt at self-promotion was dubbed Grateful Dead Records and its first release was *Wake of the Flood,* which features two classics, "Stella Blue" and "Eyes of the World."

Q As the band had learned in the "Skullfuck" debacle, distributors and retail chains could be just as much a pain in the tie-dye as record company executives. What was their initial plan to get around these pesky entities?

A Their tour manager, Ron Rakow, came up with a plan to distribute records directly to consumers from converted ice cream trucks. He also thought it would be a great scam to finance the startup of Grateful Dead Records with a small-business loan from the federal government. Predictably, neither concept panned out.

Q Finish the verse:
Wake up to find out
That you are the eyes of the world . . .

A *. . . but the heart has its beaches/its homeland and thoughts of its own.*

Q The Grateful Dead had always obsessed over the quality of their performance sound system, and by 1974 it had grown so large that it had acquired a nickname. What was it? And to demonstrate your absolute mastery of Grateful Dead trivia, how many speakers did that 1974 system contain? (You get the point if your answer is within 10.)

A At least one book has been written just about the "Wall of Sound." It contained 604 speakers in total, and sucked 26,400 watts of power through a military-surplus shore power line designed for ships. The whole array was 85 feet wide, which made it hard to fit onto some stages. The point of all that juice wasn't so much loudness as clarity; with so much amplification, none of the equipment had to work anywhere near capacity, which minimized distortion to almost nothing. It was quite a setup for a band that once had made do with two extension cords.

Q Where can you see the Wall of Sound?

A Its construction is the focus of a section of *The Grateful Dead Movie.*

Between sets at a number of Dead shows in 1974, Phil Lesh and collaborator Ned Lagin teamed up to present an atonal composition that involved computers, synthesizers, and a lot of weird improvisation. The piece later appeared on a record that included luminaries such as Jerry Garcia, Grace Slick, and David Crosby. What was it called?

Seastones.

How was the Dead's October 20, 1974 gig at the Winterland in San Francisco billed?

"The Last One." It was the final show of a five-night series that the band filmed for use in a concert movie Garcia wanted to produce. After the shows, the Dead had announced they were going to take a nice long break; in fact, they didn't say how long they were breaking for, which fueled rumors that the band might be going into permanent retirement. They had, after all, been playing together for ten long years, and a Grateful Dead show, once an impromptu happening, now required all the personnel and logistical support of a small military operation. They had never sought the big time, and they had had enough of it.

Q How long did the band's retirement last? And for extra long, strange points, where and when did they make their first post-hiatus appearance?

A They were out for nearly two years. During most of that time, Jerry Garcia was absorbed in making *The Grateful Dead Movie*, and his dedication to perfection and experimentation created all the usual delays. The band resumed touring on June 3, 1976, at the Paramount Theater in Portland, Oregon.

Q What was the live album that came out of the same 1974 Winterland shows that produced *The Grateful Dead Movie*?

A *Steal Your Face,* the cover of which features the logo Bear had commissioned for the band's gear cases. As a result, many fans have dubbed the lightening skull logo "Steal Your Face" ever since.

Q What was the Legion of Mary? (Hint: You need two answers to get full points on this one.)

A It was (and is) the largest lay Catholic organization in the world, whose millions of members gather to pray and do good works. It was also the name of Jerry Garcia's 1974 side project, along with organist Merl Saunders, bassist John Kahn, drummer Paul Humphrey, and Martin Fierro on woodwinds. Ron Tutt soon replaced Humphrey at the drum kit. The Legion was Jerry's chance during the Dead's hiatus to play a wide variety of music—everything from jazz to reggae—mostly in small clubs in the Bay Area. The original Legion of Mary gigged for about a year before Garcia and Saunders parted ways; the rest of the band reformulated to become the first iteration of the Jerry Garcia Band in 1975.

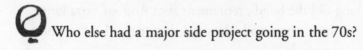

Q Who else had a major side project going in the 70s?

A Bob Weir, who joined the band Kingfish in 1974. Formed around the musical partnership of guitarist Matthew Kelly and bassist Dave Torbert, Kingfish had a more characteristic '70s sound than the Grateful Dead; it was funky, polished music with an R&B flavor. They made a perfect opening act for bands like the Eagles, Elton John, and Aerosmith, and Weir's notoriety helped them build enough of a following that they were soon headlining themselves. They managed to make an album in 1977 with Weir; but when the Grateful Dead started touring again, Bob had less and less time to devote to Kingfish. Torbert kept Kingfish rolling on, however, until, after the end of the Grateful Dead in 1995, he rejoined Weir to form Ratdog.

Q *Great North Special, were you on board?/You can't find a ride like that no more.* What are Hunter and Garcia talking about in their song, "Might as Well?"

A The Trans Canadian Pop Tour, a weeklong series of shows that crossed the continent in 1970. Not only were some great acts along—the Dead, Traffic, Janis Joplin, Buddy Guy—but they made the trip in a luxury passenger train. The rolling party and jam session that resulted became the stuff of legend.

Q During that "one long party from front to end," Delaney Bramlett of Delaney and Bonnie was jamming with Jerry Garcia on the train and taught him a traditional hard-luck road song that would become a concert standard for the Grateful Dead. They often paired it with "Not Fade Away." Sing the chorus.

A *Goin' down the road, feelin' bad*
Goin' down the road, feelin' bad
Goin' down the road, feeling bad, oh Lord
And I ain't gonna be treated this a-way.

Q Name the song; and for extra Bird of Paradise points, for whom was it written?
Arabian wind
The Needle's Eye is thin
The Ships of State sail on mirage
And drown in sand
Out in No-man's Land...

A These are the opening lines of the Hunter-Garcia song "Blues for Allah," an experimental suite that appears on the 1975 album of the same name. Hunter says he wrote the lyrics as a requiem for Saudi King Faisal, who was assassinated that year and who was (of course!) a Deadhead.

Q *Blues for Allah* was one of the Grateful Dead's most popular albums. Was the song a great success in concert?

A No; with this composition, the band had out-innovated itself. "Oh, that song was a bitch to do!" Garcia was quoted as saying. "It was not of this world. It's not in any key and it's not in any time." As a result, the band only performed the suite live five times in 1975, and then gave up on it.

Q John Barlow's lyrics sound like they're describing a band we all know and love. What song are they from?
They're a band beyond description
Like Jehovah's favorite choir
People joining hand in hand
While the music plays the band
Lord, they're setting us on fire…

A "The Music Never Stopped," Barlow's composition with Bob Weir, also on the *Blues for Allah* album.

Q By 1975, Grateful Dead Records was, essentially, defunct. What classic bit of larceny ended the band's stint as record company execs?

A As part of the deal that got *The Grateful Dead Movie* made, the band had promised five albums to United Artists' record division. Grateful Dead Records president Ron Rakow tried to insert himself in the negotiations, and his loony business style impressed no one. He was also pressing to complete the *Steal Your Face* album for UA, despite the general consensus of the Dead that the lousy concert recordings could not be salvaged. The band decided to fire him, whereupon he wrote himself checks for the balance of GDR's bank accounts and took off (as with Lenny Hart's embezzlement, Garcia and company never prosecuted Rakow). Their record company was bankrupt, they had other recording obligations, and the Grateful Dead were out of the record business.

Q Name the albums the Grateful Dead released on their own record label. Extra hippies-in-suits points if you can name the years of their release.

A *Wake of the Flood* (1974), *Grateful Dead from the Mars Hotel* (1974), *Blues for Allah* (1975).

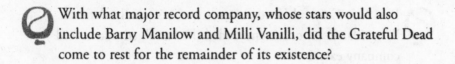

Q With what major record company, whose stars would also include Barry Manilow and Milli Vanilli, did the Grateful Dead come to rest for the remainder of its existence?

A That would be Arista Records, a subsidiary of Columbia founded by former CBS Records executive Clive Davis in 1974.

Q Which studio albums did the Grateful Dead release on Arista Records?

A Some of their most and least successful, at least from the standpoint of sales: *Terrapin Station* (1977), *Shakedown Street* (1978), *Go to Heaven* (1980), *In the Dark* (1987), and *Built to Last* (1989).

Q Complete the verse, and then translate your answer into English:
Hey now (hey now)
Hey now (hey now)
Iko iko un day . . .

A *Jockomo feeno ah na nay/Jokomo feena nay.* And, of course, there isn't any real translation. The lyrics for "Iko Iko" come from a chant used by the Mardi Gras Indian "tribes," and while there's no literal meaning, the intent was always clear enough: It was one of many mock-voodoo spells used to taunt rival parade tribes. Many performers have covered the song, most notably the Dixie Cups, who had a hit with it in 1964. The Dead began performing the song in concert in 1977, and it was another popular sing-along number in their sets.

Q In the old English folk ballad that bears her name, what item does the Lady of Carlisle use to create trouble between rival suitors? And what the heck does that have to do with the Grateful Dead?

A You know the answers if you remember the lyrics to the Hunter-Garcia song, "Terrapin Station," from the 1977 Dead album of the same name. Hunter used the old song as inspiration for his version; in both, the lady tosses her fan in a lion's den to see which of her potential boyfriends, a soldier and a sailor, will go in after it. The soldier passes; the sailor retrieves the fan and gets the girl. While the traditional ballad makes it clear that the sailor is the better of the two men, Hunter's lyrics retain the Dead's typical moral ambiguity: *The sailor coming out again/the lady fairly leapt at him/that's how it stands today/ you decide if he was wise . . ."*

Q What's the most unusual venue the Grateful Dead ever played?

A It would be harder to find anyplace more unusual for a rock concert than the Great Pyramid of Giza outside Cairo, Egypt, but for the Dead, it was a natural. The band had long wanted to play an exotic location, and Garcia and Lesh were intrigued by "power spots" like pyramids ever since they had visited Stonehenge in 1972. In 1978, they arranged to play a series of open-air September shows on a stage at the famous Sphinx, with the proceeds going to charity. The shows weren't much musically, but Garcia and company had a fine time exploring the Great Pyramid and getting to know the local villagers.

Q Shortly into their first show in Egypt, Phil Lesh had a vision of hundreds of bats swarming around his head. What was responsible for that weird trip?

A Hundreds of bats were swarming around his head. The stage lights had attracted clouds of mosquitoes from the nearby Nile, and the old stage itself was home to the winged mammals. When their favorite snack arrived, the bats flew out from under the stage and ate their fill. It certainly wasn't the weirdest experience the band had ever had on stage, and the show went on.

Q What cosmic event marked their third pyramid performance?

A For an extra-trippy coda to their Egypt experience, their third evening show was marked by a total eclipse of the moon.

Q What song from the 1978 album *Shakedown Street* provided a magic charm for Deadheads?

A The Bob Weir/John Barlow collaboration, "I Need a Miracle." The boogie shuffle with its sing-along title line became a concert favorite, and led to a piece of Deadhead lore: If you showed up at a Dead show without a ticket, repeating the line "I need a miracle" aloud would make one come to you.

Q Where was Shakedown Street?

A Outside of any Grateful Dead concert venue. It was the name for the row of white-tented vending stands where Deadheads sold various curios and glad-rags to finance their pilgrimage with the band.

Q The cover art on *Shakedown Street* should look familiar to underground comics fans. Who drew it?

A Gilbert Shelton, creator of *The Fabulous Furry Freak Brothers*.

Q By 1978, the Godchauxes were on their way out, and the Grateful Dead once again needed a new keyboard player. Name the individual who next tickled the keys for them.

A Brent Mydland, a Bay Area musician who caught the attention of Bob Weir during Arista sessions with the country rock band Silver. Bob invited Brent to join the Bob Weir Band; when that group toured with the Jerry Garcia Band in 1977, Garcia was also taken with Mydland's combination of technical excellence and soulful feel. As Keith Godchaux began melting down, Garcia suggested that they recruit Brent as a replacement. After a few months of listening to Dead tapes and rehearsing with the band, Brent began performing with the Dead in concert in 1979.

Mydland grew up in suburban Contra Costa County in California. Where was he born?

  Munich, Germany, where his father was stationed as a U.S. Army chaplain. Brent was born in 1952, which made him young enough to have grown up on Grateful Dead music; and indeed, Pigpen was one of his influences as he transitioned from his early classical piano training to rock keyboards.

Did the new guy work out?

 Oh, yeah, man. There was the inevitable learning curve, of course—"He was used to playing songs with beginnings, middles, and ends," recalled Mickey Hart—but once Mydland settled down he brought a revitalized sound to the road-worn band. In a way, his keyboard work combined the best elements of all his predecessors; he had the chops and musical breadth of Constanten and Godchaux and the soul of Pigpen. His backing vocals added strength to the band's harmonies, and he could even do solid lead vocals. If those contributions weren't sufficient, he was a terrific songwriter and brought a new ear to selecting fresh cover material as well.

Identify the traditional Mardi Gras song Mydland brought to the band that became a concert favorite when the Dead began performing it in the late 1980s.

 "Hey Pocky Way," which was born among the black Mardi Gras Indian tribe the Wild Tchoupitoulas, and played as a rocking soul number by bands like the Meters and the Neville Brothers.

Q Identify both titles of this song:
Never trust a woman who wears her pants too tight
She might love you tomorrow
But she'll be gone tomorrow night.

A "Never Trust a Woman" is also known as "Good Times"
(for the opening line, *Gonna see some good times*). This is one
of Brent Mydland's songs that got him a reputation among
some fans as a misogynist (although it's mild by comparison
with some of Pigpen's material).

They may have been showing more than a touch of gray, but the Grateful Dead were on the verge of their greatest popularity in 1985.

CHAPTER SIX

So Many Roads

As the New Wave-yuppie-Ronald Reagan '80s dawned, you would have been justified in pegging the Grateful Dead as the walking dead, a lumbering musical dinosaur whose time had passed a decade earlier. You would, of course, have been Dead wrong. The band was a bright spot of tie-dyed color in a world of earth-tone suits, a reminder in the midst of the "Greed is Good" era that there was really nothing funny about peace, love, and understanding. A new generation of young people joined the Grateful Dead caravan, and brought the band a level of popularity and financial success it had never before achieved.

But despite their fans' demand to re-create the lost golden realm of hippiedom at every show, the Grateful Dead never became an oldies act. New members brought new influences, the experiments with new music and technology continued, great new songs filled the air, and the band remained committed to its unique take on life and music. If the pressures of success, the corrosion of burnout, and the ravages of age made the magic appear less frequently, it could still be found at a Dead show.

And it still can, even more than a dozen years since the death of Jerry Garcia. New collections of the band's live recordings continue to appear; the surviving band members themselves continue to perform together and in their own side projects; and new bands have taken up the improvisational approach to live performance that the Dead pioneered. The Grateful Dead have left an enduring legacy to American popular music—here's hoping the music never stops.

Q They were responsible for the Grateful Dead's endurance as a band; but as the 1980s rolled on, they became a major headache as well, causing the band to reject venues and cancel shows. Who were these mixed blessings?

A Deadheads. Because of the unique ambiance at a Dead concert, and because no two shows were ever the same, the band had always attracted regular fans who attended show after show. With its various fan club activities and newsletters, the Dead had encouraged a close relationship with its devotees. By the 1980s, however, the hoard of fans following the band from show to show had achieved critical mass, and a number of self-sustaining commercial enterprises (T-shirts, jewelry, etc.) developed to serve it. Tent cities began forming days before the show, and thousands of Deadheads gathered, many with no chance of actually getting tickets to the sold-out concerts. Various mind-expanding substances were freely vended and consumed. As a result, many communities made themselves off-limits for Dead concerts; security became a major concern, and occasional incidents of crime and injury led the band itself to make several attempts to prohibit camping outside venues.

Q Where did the term "Deadhead" first appear?

A On the sleeve of the band's 1971 live album, *Grateful Dead*, also known as *Skull & Roses* for its cover art. "Dead Heads" was part of the address to which the band invited fans to write.

Q According to a joke among the Grateful Dead family, how can you identify a Deadhead?

A "He's still here."

Q What's the Deadhead uniform?

A Dude! Tie-dye, of course.

Q Then there are the subclassifications of Deadheads. Who are "spinners"?

A They're the ones spinning around and around at concerts. Spinners take their spinning very seriously; it's a form of meditation, similar to the whirling of Sufi dervishes. Some spinners are members of a sect known as The Church of Unlimited Devotion, which uses Grateful Dead music in worship services.

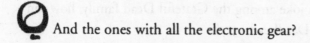

Q And the ones with all the electronic gear?

A The Tapers. While attempting to tape a performance will get you thrown out of many concerts, the Grateful Dead encouraged the practice, and made prime acoustic space available for fans to set up their microphones.

Q There's even a group of Deadheads in recovery from substance abuse. What's the name of the song from the *Skull & Roses* album that this group adopted?

A They're called the Warf Rats, after the Hunter-Garcia song about a broken down wino looking for a new start.

Q What do Bill Clinton, Ann Coulter, Al Frankin, and Tucker Carlson all have in common?

A That's right, man. Heads. Tony Blair, Al and Tipper Gore, and Senator Pat Leahy, too. As the Deadhead motto says, "We're Everywhere."

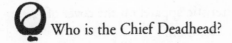 Who is the Chief Deadhead?

There may be other pretenders to the title, but it truly belongs to musician and Dead historian David Gans. Gans started writing about the Dead for music magazines in the 1970s, and began hosting a Berkeley radio show devoted to the band, *The Grateful Dead Hour.* With the band's rise in popularity in the late '80s, the show became syndicated nationally, and brought live Grateful Dead music to millions who had never heard it before. Gans has written five books about the Dead—one of which was translated into Italian—and was part of the team that compiled the rarity tracks on the *Golden Road* box set.

What second-set staple did Jerry Garcia call "just free form music—it's not rhythmic, it's not really attached to any musical norms—it's the completely weird shit"?

"Space," the nightly improvisation of electronic sounds, eclectic rhythm instruments, and noodling around on guitars. The band would often choose a theme from current events around which to paint their experimental picture.

What 38-second mix of rhythm and noise did Mickey Hart and Bill Kreutzmann contribute to the *Go to Heaven* album?

"Antwerp's Placebo (The Plumber)," a fragment reminiscent of the long "Drumz/Space" improvisations the band would create in concert. The subtitle may be attributable to the didgeridoo-like tone that sounds like a plumber's snake working a drain.

Q The Dead sported uncharacteristic apparel on the cover of *Go to Heaven*. What did they have on?

A White disco suits. It was an appropriate look for the cover of an album many felt was too slick. But hey, it was 1980, and America had just awakened from its long disco nightmare.

Q Who delivers this stinging personal assessment?
You may be Saturday's child all grown
Moving with a pinch of grace
You may be a clown in the buying ground
Or just another pretty face
You may be the fate of Ophelia
Sleeping and perchance to dream—
Honest to the point of recklessness
Self-centered to the extreme

A Althea, whose intervention-like criticism is served up in the Hunter-Garcia song that bears her name.

Q Which song from *Go to Heaven* includes the refrain, *Rain fallin' down/Rain fallin' down?*

A "Saint of Circumstance," a Bob Weir/John Barlow collaboration. One of the classic lines from this song must have seemed particularly apt at this point in the band's career: *I'm still walkin', so I'm sure that I can dance.*

Q In 1984, the Grateful Dead founded their own charitable foundation. What is it called, and how can worthy organizations apply for a grant?

A The Dead had always been generous to good causes, playing hundreds of benefit concerts over the years; but the logistics and negotiatons of dealing with too many organizations got to be a hassle. So they founded the Rex Foundation, to which proceeds from their shows could be donated and which would enable the band to decide who would get grants. It continues on today, benefiting such diverse groups as the AIDS Information Network, the Duke Ellington School of the Arts, and the Wild Dolphin Project. And there is no application process: Band members seek out causes on their own and the foundation makes grants without being asked.

Q For whom is the Rex Foundation named?

A Grateful Dead crew member Rex Jackson, an untamed spirit who died in a car accident in 1976.

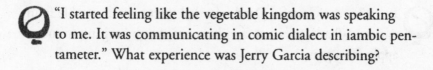

Q "I started feeling like the vegetable kingdom was speaking to me. It was communicating in comic dialect in iambic pentameter." What experience was Jerry Garcia describing?

A The experience of slipping into a coma, which he did in July, 1986. With his prodigious consumption of illegal substances, Jerry was disinclined to visit a doctor; as a result, he was unaware that he had developed type 2 diabetes, which had dehydrated him until his blood had turned to a thick sludge. While Jerry lost touch with reality, hallucinating wildly, he was still capable of fighting with the medical technicians who were trying to determine the cause of his problem. To calm him down, they injected him with Valium, to which he was allergic. Jerry's heart stopped, and he needed a defibrillator and 48 hours on a respirator before he could breathe on his own. While the incident almost claimed his life, his diabetes was discovered and treated, and his health began to improve.

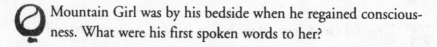

Q Mountain Girl was by his bedside when he regained consciousness. What were his first spoken words to her?

A "I'm not Beethoven."

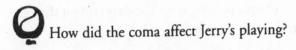

Q How did the coma affect Jerry's playing?

A Pretty severely; for a while, he forgot how to play any of his songs. But old pals like Mickey Hart, Merl Saunders, and John Kahn helped him through, playing old songs over and over as Garcia gradually recovered his musical memory. By October 1986, he was back on stage again.

Q In 1987, the Dead played six memorable concerts with an icon of rock music. Who was this individual, whose music Garcia once distained?

A Bob Dylan. As a convert from folk to rock himself, Jerry had long forgiven Dylan for his musical apostasy, and the Dead got plenty of time to hang around with him as their 1986 summer tours followed each other through America. In January 1987, they started jamming, decided to tour together, and began rehearsing in earnest in May.

Q Those six July shows produced a live album. What's its name?

A *Dylan and the Dead*, released on Columbia Records in 1989.

Q There's an extra set of eyes peering from the darkness on the *In the Dark* cover. Who do they belong to?

A Producer Bill Graham, who had showed up at the studio to complain about concert arrangements at the same time the Dead were doing the cover shoot. They worked him into the shot.

Q Finish the verse:
You imagine me sipping champagne from your boot
For a taste of your elegant pride . . .

A *I may be going to hell in a bucket, babe/But at least I'm enjoying the ride.* The Weir-Barlow composition "Hell in a Bucket" appears on the *In the Dark* album.

Q Which song on *In the Dark* is often interpreted as referring to the death of comedian John Belushi?

A "West L.A. Fadeaway". The song's opening lines are *Looking for a chateau/Twenty-one rooms but one will do,* and it was easy to hear a reference to the Chateau Marmont on the Sunset Strip where the star of *Animal House* made his final fadeaway in 1982.

Q Which song on *In the Dark* is based on a story in the Book of Genesis? And for extra apocalypse points, what is the name of the person from whose point of view the lyrics are written?

R "My Brother Esau," whose story is told in Genesis chapters 25, 27, and 33. And that would make the singer Esau's younger brother, Jacob. In the story, the eldest brother is his father Issac's favorite; the jealous Jacob cheats him of his inheritance.

Q What was the Grateful Dead's only Top Ten hit?

R The survival anthem, "A Touch of Grey", released in 1987. It topped out at No. 9 on the Billboard charts, and its success helped propel *In the Dark* to become the only Grateful Dead album to go platinum on release.

Q It was the 1980s, after all, and you couldn't very well have a hit record without a music video. The one the Dead made for "A Touch of Grey" turned out to be one of MTV's most requested. What was the video's visual gimmick?

R Life-sized skeleton puppets that stand in for band members, playing instruments and singing, while an auditorium crowd cheers on. The Bill Kreutzmann puppet smokes a cigarette, and the Bob Weir puppet catches a rose in its teeth. The effect was designed by Gary Gutierrez, who had done the incredible animation for *The Grateful Dead Movie*. Check it out on YouTube, man.

Q What otherworldly singers did Mickey Hart introduce to America with a 1987 album he produced?

A The Gyuto Monks, a choir of twenty specially trained singers who make up the Dalai Lama's personal tantric choir.

Q What makes the singing of the Gyuto Monks unique?

A They have learned to shape their vocal cavities to do the seemingly impossible: produce a three-note major chord with a single voice. Hearing one of them chant this way is amazing; to hear the incredible shifting wave forms produced by twenty monks singing together is to be instantly transported to a transcendental realm.

Q What was the highly appropriate name of the Grateful Dead's final studio album?

A *Built to Last*, recorded and released in 1989. Its cover photo shows the band members collaborating on an elaborate house of cards.

Q Complete Robert Hunter's musical proverb:
Crown yourself the king of clowns
Or stand way back apart
But never give your love, my friend . . .

A *. . . unto a foolish heart.* First performed in 1988, "Foolish Heart" appears on the *Built to Last* album.

Q Identify the song, and who wrote it:
Little girl lost
In a forest of dreams
It's a dark old wood
And it's damp with dew
Hoot owl hoots
For a moment it seems
Something big and cold
Just got hold of you.

A These are the opening lines of "I Will Take You Home," from the *Built to Last* album. Its composition was a collaboration between John Barlow (who was Bob Weir's usual lyricist) and Brent Mydland.

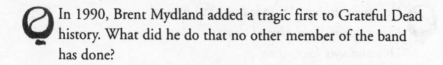

Q In 1990, Brent Mydland added a tragic first to Grateful Dead history. What did he do that no other member of the band has done?

A He died of a drug overdose. While it could be argued persuasively that substance abuse contributed heavily to the deaths of all three Grateful Dead members who have passed to the Great Gig in the Sky, only Brent's death was directly attributable to dope. Despite his musical genius, Mydland had a depressive personality, and he turned to alcohol and drugs for self-medication. A combination of drug busts and DUI arrests had congealed into a pending jail stint; he chose the reaper over the jailer, and died in his home in Lafayette, California, on July 26, shortly after the end of the band's summer tour.

Q What specific drug cocktail killed Brent Mydland?

A An injected mixture of morphine and cocaine known as a "speedball."

Q What other famous performers died the same way?

A Speedballs also killed television and film stars John Belushi in 1982 and Chris Farley in 1997 (although junk connoisseurs may note that the opiate in their terminal highs was heroin).

Q Who replaced Brent Mydland as the Grateful Dead's last keyboardist?

A On keyboards for the Dead from 1990 to 1995 was Vince Welnick. Like Mydland, Welnick was born in the 1950s, and saw his first Grateful Dead show in 1970 when he was 19. Prior to his stint with the Dead, his most notable work had been with the '70s rock fusion act, the Tubes, whose first single was the memorably titled "Don't Touch Me There." Despite the Tubes' flashy, trashy vibe, Welnick's jazz chops and devotion to artists like John Coltrane made him a great fit for this band of aging hippies.

Q On what Tubes hit did Welnick perform?

A The one you can probably sing the chorus to is their 1977 hit, "White Punks on Dope."

Q In what piece of classic '70s bad cinema do the Tubes appear?

A You can see them in Olivia Newton-John's disco opus, *Xanadu*.

Q The last album released by the Grateful Dead during Jerry Garcia's lifetime appeared in 1990. Name it.

A The live album, *Without a Net*.

Q It could be argued that the "acid jazz" genre was born in a series of 1990 Grateful Dead shows. Who was the legendary jazzman that jammed with the band?

A Saxophonist Branford Marsalis. Phil Lesh had been a fan of his work with Art Blakey's Jazz Messengers and his brother Winton Marsalis's band, and got to know him; Phil was surprised and delighted to learn that Branford wanted to sit in with the Dead. He first joined the band on stage on March 29, 1990, and his horn clicked so well with Jerry's guitar that they played four more concerts with Branford that year.

Q On what song from the *Without a Net* live album can you hear Branford Marsalis playing with the band?

A That's his soprano saxophone on "Eyes of the World," the second song he ever played with the Grateful Dead.

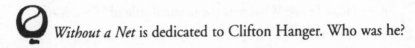

Q *Without a Net* is dedicated to Clifton Hanger. Who was he?

A Clifton Hanger was a pseudonym used by Brent Mydland when he didn't want to use his real name in hotel guest registers. Mydland died during the album's production.

Q Name the song:
I turn on Channel Six, the President comes on the news
Says I got no satisfaction, that's why I sing the blues
His wife says don't get crazy, Lord, you know just what to do
Just crank up that old Victrola, put on your rocking shoes.

A "One More Saturday Night," a Bob Weir composition that he wrote in 1971. It appears on the *Without a Net* live album.

Q Given the year of the song's composition, who would the conversation recorded in these lines have occurred between?

A The 37th president of the United States, Richard Milhous Nixon, and his wife, Pat. Picture that, man.

Q Super Head Level: What was the original title of "One More Saturday Night?"

A You know your stuff if you know that Bob Weir wanted to call his song "U.S. Blues." Robert Hunter had played with lyrics for the Uncle Sam song, then let the concept lapse. Hunter also wrote the initial lyrics for "One More Saturday Night," and was unhappy with Weir's rewrite of them. When Weir wanted to call the song "U.S. Blues," Hunter refused to allow it, and eventually disavowed any connection with "One More Saturday Night."

Q Mickey Hart released a book and an album in 1991 that shared the same title. What was it?

A Both projects, part of Mickey's ongoing effort to illuminate the importance of rhythm to human culture, were entitled *Planet Drum*. The album features a cast of percussion virtuosos from around the world playing just about everything you can hit with a stick.

Q Bob Weir and his sister, Wendy, also put out a book in 1991. What's it called?

A The children's book, featuring Bob's original story and Wendy's illustrations, was entitled *Panther Dream*. Proceeds from the book were devoted to rainforest and education projects in Africa.

Q In 1994, Phil Lesh got to live one of his lifelong dreams. What was it?

A The inveterate "air conductor" got to do the real thing as a guest conductor for the Berkeley Symphony. True to his experimentalist groove, Lesh led the orchestra through a movement of Stravinsky's *Firebird Suite* and a piece by composer Eliot Carter entitled *A Celebration of Some 100 x 150 Notes.*

Q Where and when was the Grateful Dead's last show?

A July 9, 1995, at Soldier Field, Chicago. It was the end of a summer tour that had so many problems that crew members circulated the rumor that it was cursed. Attempts to control the army of Deadheads following the band met with limited success; in St. Louis, a crowd of fans were crammed onto a porch roof that collapsed, sending more than 100 to the hospital. There were death threats and violence; crew members were fighting, and Garcia's physical and mental state continued to deteriorate.

Q What was the Deadhead Riot?

A At the Deer Creek Music Center in Indiana in July 1995, a gate-crashing incident sparked a riot in which Deadheads literally tore the place apart; the next day's show had to be canceled.

Q What was the last song Jerry Garcia ever recorded?

A The Jimmie Rogers song, "Blue Yodel #9." On July 13, Jerry went to David Grisman's studio to record the number as a contribution to a tribute album to the country music pioneer. Grisman recalls he was in good spirits, but looked terrible and seemed to be short-winded, which of course caused problems with yodeling.

Q Where did Jerry Garcia spend the last few weeks of his life?

A In rehab. His struggles to keep it together during the 1995 tour convinced him that he had to do something about his drug and alcohol problems. He started out at the famous Betty Ford Clinic for two weeks. After a brief interlude at home, punctuated by visits to Alcoholics Anonymous meetings and a recovery psychologist, he checked into a substance abuse clinic on August 8.

Q Where and when did Jerry Garcia die? And what killed him?

A Jerry took his final trip sometime in the early hours of August 9, 1995. A nurse at Serenity Knolls, the substance abuse clinic near Lagunitas, found him dead at 4:23 a.m. It wasn't drugs that killed him; it was a heart attack, probably aggravated by chronic sleep apnea, another health problem he'd ignored for years.

Q Where are Jerry's remains?

A Most of Jerry's ashes were spread on the waters of San Francisco Bay; but a small portion was scattered in the Ganges River in India.

Q A year after Jerry's death, two members of the Grateful Dead were touring together. To get full points on this question, you have to name the tour and identify the nickname widely used for it.

A What eventually came to be called the Further Festival, named after the Merry Pranksters bus, was originally dubbed "Deadapalooza," echoing the Lollapalooza all-star tour. But the Grateful Dead weren't there. The band had quickly decided never to use the name again; beside that, Bob Weir and Mickey Hart had announced the tour without telling Phil Lesh, who was incensed at the idea.

Q Name the all-star lineup of acts at the Further Festival.

A The concerts featured Ratdog, Mickey Hart's Mystery Box, Los Lobos, Hot Tuna, the Flying Karamazov Brothers, and jazz pianist Bruce Hornsby.

Q Ratdog is the latest of Bob Weir's collaborations without the Grateful Dead. What other bands has he played with?

A Besides touring with Kingfish in the mid-70s, there was the Bob Weir Band that also featured Dead keyboardist Brent Mydland; Weir also fronted a group called Bobby and the Midnighters.

Q How well did the band keep their vow to retire the Grateful Dead name?

A They're at 50 percent. In 1998, Lesh, Weir, Hart, and Kreutzmann picked up some side musicians and started touring again as The Other Ones. But the Dead was the Dead, after all, and that's the name that the group toured as in 2003 and 2004.

Q Phil Lesh had some major health problems of his own in 1998. What was the problem, and what procedure was required?

A Phil had struggled with Hepatitis C, probably contracted from a drug needle and aggravated by alcohol consumption. By the late '90s he was living the clean life, but he experienced sudden weight loss and suffered an internal hemorrhage in September '98 that caused him to collapse. His liver was on the verge of failure, and only a transplant would save him. Thanks to the operation he recovered fully, and he's been an outspoken advocate of organ donation ever since.

Q Many musicians have toured with Phil Lesh and Friends. Two in particular represented a link with the Grateful Dead's musical legacy. Name them.

A Trey Anastasio and Page McConnell of Phish, the band that reinterpreted the live long-form improvisation for the grunge generation. Many say that the rise of Phish in the mid-1990s is directly attributable to the absence of the Grateful Dead after Jerry Garcia's death.

Q Who are the Rhythm Devils? And where did they get their name?

A Mickey Hart, Bill Kreutzmann, former Phish bassist Mike Gordon, and The Other Ones lead guitarist Steve Kimock toured as the Rhythm Devils in 2006, including in their repertoire new songs by Robert Hunter. It's the nickname Hart and Kreutzmann created for themselves when they first started playing together in 1967.

Q In 1987, *In the Dark* was the only Grateful Dead album to sell more than 10 million copies, and thus go "Double Platinum," upon release. But the enduring popularity of the band helped two other Dead albums reach the Double Platinum mark by 2001. Which ones?

A You might have guessed that *American Beauty* was one of them. The other was the live compilation of the Grateful Dead's 1972 European tour, *Europe '72*.

Q 2001 also saw Gold certification for a massive Grateful Dead re-release. What was it?

A The enormous box set, *The Golden Road (1965-1973)*, a 12-CD compilation that retailed for a hefty $150. But it's a real treasure: along with every album the Dead released by 1973, it contains all kinds of special unreleased treats, including their very first studio recordings. It has all the original cover art and the standard box set booklet, and the recordings are all lovingly remastered to sound better than they ever have. The fact that so many fans have been willing to pay so much to buy the set, which contains a lot of music they already own, is a true indicator of the band's undiminished popularity.

Q Rhino Records, which released *The Golden Road*, gave the same kind of big box treatment to the Dead's material from the '70s and '80s in 2004. What was it called?

A *Beyond Description (1973-1989)*.

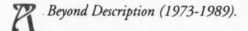

Q The Grateful Dead may own the title of the most prolific defunct rock band, thanks to two series of live recording releases. What are their names?

A *Dick's Picks* and the *From the Vault* series, both released by Grateful Dead Records, and both drawn from the band's massive archive of live concert recordings.

Q What's the main difference between the two live series?

A The *Vault* series, of which there have been four releases to date, is based on multi-track recordings and is considered to have the better sound quality of the two. All four have been released in combination packages with DVDs of performance footage. *Dick's Picks* is based on two-track sound check tapes, which means the sound quality can be less reliable, but there is a lot more material available: 36—count 'em, 36—volumes in the *Dick's Picks* series had been released by 2005.

Q Who is the Dick in *Dick's Picks?*

A Dick Latvala, the band's official sound archivist, who produced the albums under their supervision until his death in 1999. The series continues under the Dead's current archivist, David Lemieux.

Q And Grateful Dead Records has not ignored the new media. What exclusive music is available only through the Grateful Dead online store?

A Downloads, and lots of them. In addition to offering the entire Grateful Dead Records catalog and many other CDs, the band's official website, www.dead.net, has the *Download Series,* which includes 13 digital files of live performances.

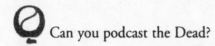

Q Can you podcast the Dead?

R Totally. *The Grateful Dead Hour* is available for download at www.gdhour.com, and there are at least two other sources for regular Dead podcasts available (just Google it, man).

Q What new source of digital Dead appeared in 2007?

R The Sirius satellite radio network premiered a channel devoted exclusively to the Grateful Dead, featuring live concert recordings and interviews with band members.

Q What do Widespread Panic, Aquarium Rescue Unit, the Disco Biscuits, Of a Revolution, and String Cheese Incident have in common?

R They've all been given the sobriquet, "jam band." Although jam bands play many different styles of music, they share a desire to explore the kind of extended improvisational performance techniques that the Grateful Dead pioneered for rock music. Jam music started in the mid-1980s and is still going strong two decades later. If that phenomenon alone wasn't enough to cement the Grateful Dead's legacy to popular music, the many Dead tribute acts committed to preserving the band's concert sound certainly would. Somewhere, Jerry is smiling.

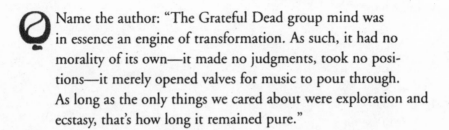 Name the author: "The Grateful Dead group mind was in essence an engine of transformation. As such, it had no morality of its own—it made no judgments, took no positions—it merely opened valves for music to pour through. As long as the only things we cared about were exploration and ecstasy, that's how long it remained pure."

Phil Lesh, in the conclusion to his 2005 autobiography, *Searching for the Sound: My Life with the Grateful Dead.* He continued, "There will never be another band like the Grateful Dead." Amen, brother.